Wedding Wisdom

An Insightful Approach to Wedding Planning

Dear Juliana + Patrick,

Wishing you
continued success
& joy at being
your BEST SELF!

XO

Mary Dann

Wedding Wisdom

An Insightful Approach to Wedding Planning

Written by Mary Dann-McNamee, M.A.,
Wedding Planner since 1991
In collaboration with Leila Khalil,
Wedding Publicist

iUniverse, Inc.
New York   Bloomington

Wedding Wisdom
An Insightful Approach to Wedding Planning

iUniverse books may be ordered through booksellers or by contacting:

iUniverse
1663 Liberty Drive
Bloomington, IN 47403
www.iuniverse.com
1-800-Authors (1-800-288-4677)

Because of the dynamic nature of the Internet, any Web addresses or links contained in this book may have changed since publication and may no longer be valid. The views expressed in this work are solely those of the author and do not necessarily reflect the views of the publisher, and the publisher hereby disclaims any responsibility for them.

ISBN: 978-1-4401-6296-1 (pbk)
ISBN: 978-1-4401-6298-5 (dj)
ISBN: 978-1-4401-6297-8 (ebk)

Printed in the United States of America

iUniverse rev. date: 10/16/2009

Contents

Accolades

"Mary's highly regarded articles and contributions over the years have provided refreshing insight and valuable information for brides and our wedding community." - *Publisher Amy Harrick, Ceremony Magazine*

"As a long time friend and colleague of Mary's, I am so grateful for her inclusive approach to wedding planning and her commitment to writing such an inspiring book. Her advice compassionately invites brides to plan for their perfect day and planners to create a balanced dream business." - *Young Song Martin, Owner of Wildflower Linen*

"Mary Dann's wisdom and excellence is captured so beautifully in this incredible 'go to' resource for planners! Mary's background uniquely equips her to guide, inspire and co-create that 'one of a kind' day that creatively expresses the essence each wedding couple wishes to convey." - *Jean Schulte, Director of Incentive Sales - KSL Resorts*

"Mary Dann offers sage advice to help other wedding planners be better at being a professional planner. She sets high standards for others to follow." - *Loreen Stevens, New York City Casting Director "Whose Wedding is it Anyway?"*

"Thankfully I hired Mary to help me plan my dream destination wedding for over 150 guests, in 4 months. Her wisdom, patience and fabulous insights were more than what I could have wished for! Her book and approach to wedding planning is not only a breath of fresh air but gift to all those choosing to plan their own wedding or be a wedding planner." - *Rosalynn Sumners, 1984 Olympic Athlete, Silver Medalist in Ice Skating and Past Bride*

Acknowledgments by Mary Dann-McNamee

"If the only prayer you ever say in your entire life is 'thank you' it will be enough...."
                                                          - Meister Eckhart

Words are not enough to express my gratitude towards my husband, Jimmy, who by his patience, love and understanding has given me the space to create, grow and flourish professionally and personally. Without him, my two precious baby girls, Sophia and Grace, would not be who they are today a slice of heaven everyday!

My sweeties, Sophia and Grace, who have inspired me to dream bigger, stay balanced along the way and give all I have.

I am very grateful for my large, colorful and diverse family members (too numerous to mention) who have planted seeds of patience, compassion and acceptance for uniqueness in me through their example. I am grateful for all the many crazy moments and experiences we've shared, which have given me a training ground to assist others through their journey of creating special memories. Most especially I am thankful for my biggest fan and best friend, my mom, Rosetta "Ronnie" Dann-Honor and Rosanne "Rose" Broghamer, who I feel extremely blessed to have as a little sister and best friend.

Thanks to my team of ladies that have helped me along the way, especially my Wedding Publicist, Leila Khalil; My event managers, Carissa Jones-Jowett, Shannon Berg, Constance Curtis, Holly Schoenke, and Stephanie Eversfield; and day-of assistants, Melissa Churlonis, Jennifer Kelley, and Deborah Anderson, PhD. In addition my intern, personal assistant, and event manager in training Jenny Chang has been an integral part of my team! Through their energy, kindness, and devotion to the art of wedding planning, each has added to my foundation so that I may grow all of our dreams.

I offer much gratitude to my vendors (and friends) who always help me to shine and surpass my clients' expectations, especially Margaret Yasuda of Mimio Papers in Pasadena, California. Along with Fabian Gracian, Level 4 International, Van Nuys, California. And of course to my clients, who challenge me to grow to be the best person I can be. After all, it has been my past clients and current clients that continue to remind me that the work I do is "unbelievable, valuable and purposeful" and to "*please* write a book." Well here you go!

Huge thanks to novice and established wedding planners across the world that send me notes of gratitude for all I do to help them grow their business and dreams. It reassures me that what I am doing is meaningful. Thank you for supporting my DVDs, counseling sessions, mentorships, stationery and now, my book. Keep sharing the gifts you learn along the way so that we may all continue to grow as a community!

Acknowledgments by Leila Khalil

Contributing to this book with Mary Dann-McNamee has been especially meaningful to me, now that I am a bride-to-be myself! For that it has been both a professionally and personally rewarding experience, for which I would first like to thank Mary for being a great mentor and friend over the years. I am eternally grateful for the strength and ability to inspire and motivate others, encouraged by my mom, Karen Reid Khalil. Through her life she has exemplified the very essence of unconditional love and its limitless boundaries.

I believe that a strong foundation, infused with heart and a steadfast set of values, is the stepping-stone in achieving your life goals. My large family with parents Charles and Karen, siblings Jacque, Monika, Kellee, and Jirard and my fiancé Tony have provided me with immeasurable support and have been an integral part of my success in my career and everyday life. To them I offer two short words that have immense depth-thank you!

Introduction - Mary Dann-McNamee's Journey

<u>From the Beginning</u>

My name is Mary Dann-McNamee. I have been a wedding and party planner since 1991. If you do not know who I am, well then allow me introduce myself. I started in the event planning business by getting on board with the Ritz-Carlton Hotel Company in the early 1990's. My background prior to this was in various industries, but more so in the food and beverage business. Before I left my Catering Sales Manager position at The Ritz-Carlton, Rancho Mirage to work as a Corporate Group Sales Manager for The Wyndham Hotel, I passed all my, then, current clients and brides over to the succeeding Ritz-Carlton Catering Manager. Two weeks after I left The Ritz-Carlton, Pam, a former bride from The Ritz-Carlton, Rancho Mirage, called me up at my home and asked me to become her personal wedding planner. I was jazzed. I did it! I, now, felt that I had been given a gift – the gift to be and independent wedding planner. Furthermore, the wedding was at a hotel that I, absolutely, loved – The Ritz Carlton. Yet, in retrospect, at the time I really had no intention of having my own company or anything like that. My plan was to work for an up-scale company and grow personally and professionally under a structured environment with a steady paycheck, insurance, and the benefits and perks that come with a luxury hotel job. Instead, I followed my heart.

You know that I accepted the position of being Pam's wedding planner. I charged $1,500 for my three-month stint (day-of services). Since I was employed by The Wyndham Hotel, I had to explain my boundaries to her. I disclosed to her that I would only be available to serve her nights and weekends. My operational resources back then were a large cell phone, which I rarely used, home office, and a fax. I did, however, continue to use all of the vendors in the desert that I already liked and knew and within a short period of time, I officially started my own company.

In starting my own company, I created business cards and started interfacing and interacting with the staff at the other hotels as well as The Ritz-Carlton, Rancho Mirage and La Quinta Resort and Spa, where I knew many of the existing staff and managers. I presented my philosophy. My reputation spoke for itself. My mission as a wedding planner was to be a collaborator, rather than a divider. I became a supporter for all my vendors, making sure they were always set up for success and I became a mediator, reducing an hour long conversation with a bride to a ten minute conversation with a Catering Manager. Both hotels were thrilled to refer me because I made it my business to make their job easier. I felt that there was a lack of professional, creative, young wedding planners in the desert area. I was confident that I could fill that void. I remembered that as a Catering Sales Manager at The Ritz-Carlton, Rancho Mirage, I would have loved to refer business to a wedding planner that I felt would do just as good of a job as I would do or better. I saw the niche in the Desert that was not yet satisfied. I thought to myself, "Hey, I want to be a person that the catering manager(s) refer clients to" I want to be the person that I wish I would have had while working as a Catering Sales Manager at the Ritz-Carlton. I want to be the wedding planner that is helpful, kind, creative, and providing more solutions than problems. I was committed to the knowledge in my and heart and my purposeful manner in knowing how to navigate a luxury hotel with the same Total Quality Management (TQM) style that The Ritz-Carlton employs in the service industry.

I am reminded that as a Catering Sales Manager at the Ritz-Carlton, Rancho Mirage, I found myself working sixty to eighty hours a week. I was working more and yet, I was earning less money than I had in my previous jobs in the industry. It was the hardest work I had ever done, but it was actually the most fun and the most rewarding work I had ever done. I came to realize that when you take a few steps backwards in your career, in the long run they amount to large steps forward.

Ironically, I never grew up reading wedding magazines or dreaming of a big fancy wedding. I was too busy being a tomboy, excelling in athletics and socializing with many friends. I was enthralled with camping, tinkering in the garage with my dad, yard work, and figuring out how both things and people operate. I was always asking questions. I was inquisitive. So the moral of the story is, – I never envisioned this career path in the bridal industry for my life. But as I know now, life will always bring you to the place you are meant to be and in turn, my experience and blessings have been more than I could have ever thought, wanted or dreamed of.

Now, back to the business – remember, simultaneously, I was the Corporate Sales Manager at the Wyndham Hotels and managing my own wedding business on the side. I did this for three years. I would estimate that I did six to ten weddings per year. And I did them in one of the most desirable wedding destinations in the country – Palm Springs, California. Most of my brides came from Los Angeles or San Diego to create a destination wedding in the desert. Oh, and did I mention that in the midst of building my business, I got married? Yes, during this time I planned my own seventy-five person, afternoon wedding. Working two jobs was what it took to get my business running, but working two jobs was not what was fueling a healthy, loving relationship with my husband. Not too surprisingly, we got divorced fourteen months later. Many of the life lessons learned during that time are contained within this book and most importantly, I realized that it is possible to pick yourself up from any situation, rise above, and come out even stronger.

One of the most important lessons I learned quickly and want to be frank with you about is that when starting my own wedding planning business, it did not pay the bills right away and it doesn't for most planners starting out. However, when starting out, working isn't necessarily about increasing the size of your pocket book, rather it's about following your passion and adding value to your event planning experience. For me, there were times that I was sad and even discouraged, but through the struggles came clarity and I realized more about myself and became an even better professional.

After that, I worked longer days and I offered my services in many different ways so that I could stay afloat. I was dedicated to learning and I donated many hours of my time with mentors, reading, and journaling. I relocated from the desert area to the city of Los Angeles. I called any and all contacts I knew in the luxury hotel industry and I let them know I had my business and I was launching it in Los Angeles. I asked if there was any way that I could shadow them (follow them around at an event). I wanted to "walk their walk" and follow them for a few hours on a Friday or Saturday night at a wedding. Generously, I was given the chance to get to know the hotels, how they operate and at the same time, they got to know how easy it was to work with me and see how eager I was to do weddings at their property. I'd like to take a quick moment to say a special thank you to Nancy Lyons, Associate Catering Director from the Ritz-Carlton, Marina Del Rey and Debra Rosenberg from Loews Santa Monica Beach Hotel. They both allowed me to shadow them early on and put me on their exclusive referral list which helped launch my business.

What has helped me get to where I am now?

I became an open book and very pliable. When I started with The Ritz-Carlton Hotel, I absorbed The Ritz-Carlton standards of TQM and enrolled in Stephen Covey's endless Time-Management courses and adopted the motto that "...We are ladies and gentlemen, serving ladies and gentlemen..."

Being a part of the service industries has helped me to discover my calling. So much about finding your niche and your "soul" purpose or your dream job. I found out that force-fitting doesn't work. You have to follow your heart and use the skills that you, innately, possess. Whether it is working with people or being creative with floral design, it is analogous to the process of finding your soul mate. Ironically, the more work and energy you put into it, the harder it is to find. For me, when it came to the point of saying "I surrender" and "Higher Power show me the way", that was the spring board to a new direction. In a sense I opened up my heart and mind to the universe. It is amazing the positive energy and support that came along the way, to give me direction, a little nudge, and a perspective that I would have never originally considered. If nothing else, this is what I want to impart to my readers.

My beliefs that inspire me!

Belief systems keep me in a very positive space, help me to remain calm in the midst of chaos, and add a lot of joy to my life. It is so important that you are connected with your soul's purpose and your source. However you get your source of energy, of light, and of love, I encourage you to take the time to get connected and find it. Whatever it is that makes your soul sing, you must focus on discovering it and create the time to slow down to nurture it. The more that you can do that for yourself or put time in your week, day, or month to do so, the more you can actually give to other people. This is the balance of being able to give to yourself and take care of your soul, so that you can actually give of yourself to others. By feeding your soul, you will be better equipped to honor your client's voice during the short time that you are impacting their lives. By surrendering and becoming open to possibilities and gifts that you would not normally expect, it is only then that doors open and new exciting things happen.

What was important while I was nursing my passion and dream business?

What I believe is really important concerning nursing your passion is to be able to take time to breathe and feel gratitude. No matter what you are doing it gets very exciting when you are doing something you really love. Therefore, it is imperative to maintain your endurance and the beauty of life by being thankful for all the moments, the days, and the hours. Even when you are in the midst of so much going on and there is so much to juggle, stop and say to yourself, "This is awesome. This is exactly what I want to be doing. Thank you." Just the feeling and the idea of saying, "Thank you." throughout the day, all adds up. The sense of gratitude adds up and it renews a person's soul. It relieves me. I know it will be relieving to you. Throughout the day I cannot tell you how many times I am in a conversation with God or I am in a space of peace and gratitude, no matter what is going on in my life.

One of the many activities to prepare anyone for their dream job is to be able to get either a life coach or a personal psychotherapist to be able to help you through the journey of getting clear with who you are. The clearer you are with yourself the more giving, kind, compassionate, and forgiving you can be to other people. I was always blessed with the gift of friends. In my early 20's I would often ask my friend, Stephanie, what she did and said when she visited her therapist. I was curious. I had never gone to a therapist and I didn't know anyone else but Stephanie who did. I guess I felt that my volumes of journals I had been keeping for years were my way of being my own therapist. After all, I grew up with the value of using my "God given talents to the best of my ability". I thought seeing therapist was like saying I could not solve a problem by myself or I was not using all my talents to the best of my ability.

Maybe I thought it was a weakness of character. Whatever, I felt that I could be my own therapist. Then in my mid 20's, a series of issues developed. My professional life was not what I had envisioned, I just broke up from a serious relationship, and my home was changing. I started questioning my future.

It was at that time I tapped into my courage and made an appointment with a female therapist. She was easy to open up to and she helped me to see patterns in my choices and behavior. She was a loving, clear, and compassionate mirror to myself. My therapist offered choices of thought and action I had not seen or noticed before.

Later, in my late 20's I saw a male life coach may not get too involved with your growing up years, family life, love live and spiritual life. They usually focus more on your professional and physical life. My life coach was helpful in creating a personal Mission statement, a business plan and helped me visualize purposeful professional path. Whereas my Therapist, helped me practice and map out my dream for more intimate and maningful relationships with family and friends.

It is because I had such a positive experience with the therapist and coach, I chose to be a therapist myself. After all, throughout my life, I remembered hearing from my friends that I should be a therapist and get paid for my good listening and advise.

A Calling to Coach

One of the main reasons why I went into psychology was primarily because I was getting pulled into couples' and their families' lives in crisis situations through my job in event planning. There were issues that were coming up for them and they would look to me for an answer, yet I felt unprepared to give sound counseling or advice. Some of the issues that would come up included:

- ❖ "Help me tell my daughter she has to eat more, she's getting too thin."
- ❖ "How do I deal with the issue of my dad who drinks too much sometimes?"
- ❖ "How do I get my fiancé to get measured for his tuxedo? He never wants to do the wedding tasks I ask him to do."

I learned very quickly that every family has a series of dysfunctional elements, and although some families have more than others, all families have issues. I have never believed in a "normal family." They all have their quirks and that is what makes them unique. I felt it necessary to go back to school to increase my education and gather information on working with families and couples. I wanted to be more helpful and have the tools to guide them. As a planner, I get pulled into such intimate situations in such a short amount of time. Thus, getting my Masters Degree in Clinical Psychology from Antioch University in 2000 helped me to be a better Wedding Planner in ways of understanding the family unit and how couples communicate. I learned how to interpret what they were saying and often times, what they were not saying. My experience as a therapist allows me to assess an issue before it ever becomes a larger problem or crisis and helps me reduce stress for my couples, allowing them to move through the planning process with greater ease. My hope is that that this book serves as a tool kit for planners to assist them as they move through the planning rite of passage with more balance and ease.

PART 1: FOUNDATION OF WISDOM: BALANCE

What is Balance?

Balance to me means feeling complete. When I am balanced I feel whole, empowered with high self-esteem, beautiful, and confident. But in life, everything should be tempered; being balanced is about having a little bit of everything and not too much of one thing. When I am out of balance, I often feel lethargic, irritable, or anxious. Once I am out of balance I can often feel angry at myself for getting there; angry for ignoring the signs that one or more aspects of my life (i.e. physical, mental, spiritual, and emotional) are being neglected. It is most important to be aware of the signs of imbalance. They are unique and different for each one of us. Some of these signs may be short temperament, sadness, over spending, eating disorders, controlling behavior, inability to sleep through the night, or over-use of alcohol or drugs.

The Four Elements of Balance

There are four components to balance and they are the physical balance, mental balance, spiritual balance and emotional balance. I am going to go through some different ways to stay balanced. Whether you are the planner coordinating the planning process for someone else, or whether you are the bride moving through your own planning experience, balance is vital.

Physical Balance

For the bride, the physical part of balance is being able to have physical stamina to be able to enjoy your amazing wedding day experience. This means making sure you eat healthy foods, drink plenty of water, exercise, rest, and participate in preventative treatments such as massages and facials, etc. The physical items above are NOT luxuries; they are necessities for preparing to participate in an extraordinary wedding day. For the planner, you will not only be on your feet for ten to fourteen hours a day, but will also carry the emotional burden of producing an exceptional day for your clients. A wedding day is "show time". It is a person's own Academy Awards experience filled with paparazzi, special gowns, lots of attention, etc. The bride and the planner are performers for all the observers and like any performer you have to practice and prepare.

If you are still procrastinating on exercising and eating right, you need to know I am just another person coming along your journey to say, "You just need to do it." There is no way around it. There are no shortcuts, pills, or easy fix. You have to "just do it" My best advice is to carve out time from your day and get it done. Start off small and with that know that it will grow to become a momentum to your regiment. Allow yourself to create more time even if you have to diversify your work out routine. At first, do twenty minutes, and then move to thirty, and on to forty five. You will get there, one baby step at a time.

Physical Self-Esteem
Feeling powerful in your own skin and in your own body will help your self-esteem. When you feel more powerful in your physical state, you will feel more self-esteem in your overall balanced state. Start thanking your body rather than criticizing it. Do not look at what your body cannot do. Look at what your body has done and what it does do, be grateful for that. Start by thanking your fingers, your legs, and your elbows. You have them and they work very hard for you. If you do not like something about your body, then do something to change it. You have choices. Physically, you can do something to change your body or mentally, you can start changing the way you think about your body. The alternative is to do nothing but complain and wish for a magical solution that never comes.

"*You are the ordinary becoming the extraordinary.*"

Mary Dann-McNamee

Mental Balance

Mental balance is my head-centered-self. It is more of my adult-self. It is the part of me that takes care of adult issues: problem solving, creative thinking, and making responsible choices. Mental balance is very much about being organized, being accountable, and following through with your word. "Mean what you say and say what you mean." One of my favorite books addressing this topic is by Don Miguel Ruiz, called *The Four Agreements*.

The four agreements are:

1. Be impeccable with your word
    Speak with integrity. Say only what you mean. Avoid using the word to speak against yourself or to gossip about others. Use the power of your word in the direction of truth and love.

2. Do not take anything personally
   Nothing others do is because of you. What others say and do is a projection of their own reality, their own dream. When you are immune to the opinions and actions of others, you won't be the victim of needless suffering.

3. Do not make assumptions
   Find the courage to ask questions and to express what you really want. Communicate with others as clearly as you can to avoid misunderstandings, sadness and drama. With just this one agreement, you can completely transform your life.

4. Always do your best
   Your best is going to change from moment to moment; it will be different when you are healthy as opposed to sick. Under any circumstance, simply do your best, and you will avoid self-judgment, self-abuse and regret.

This is my favorite book, because it easily and clearly articulates what it is to be a "grown up" or your "adult-self." Incorporating this into your life is to do yourself a big favor.

Mental balance is being able to use your skills and resources to give the right answer for somebody when they need it. If you do not have the right answer, mental balance is knowing where to find it.

Helpful Hints on Staying Organized

Some of the things that help me stay balanced in a mental capacity is making a list that is attainable everyday and checking off your items that you need to take care of.

On a daily basis I create a list of tasks that need to get done and mark the categories as "personal" and "professional".
An example would be:

June 22, 2008

Professional
Smith wedding (I usually have 5-10 wedding clients listed with several tasks to do under each client's name).
Follow up on place cards
Confirm details with florist
Etc…

Personal (I usually have 3-4 personal tasks to do in a day. If there are more to do, I will reschedule them for the next day. My limit for personal items in one day is 4 items)
Make appointment for baby's 1 year check up
Get pants hemmed

Schedule a dental appointment
Follow up with a friend to schedule a play day for my daughter

Another standard for staying organized is, if your task takes more than 30 minutes in one day, write it down on your daily calendar. This will help you carve out the time and make it more imperative to accomplish. Please do not over schedule your day on a regular basis. It only creates negative thoughts towards yourself...which leads to my next point.

Reducing Negative Thoughts
Stay away from negative thoughts that run through your mind and that tell you that you are not good enough or you do not have enough. You have to stop with the pessimistic attitude because that will keep you in a space of low self-esteem. Most "bridezillas" and "planners gone wild" are people that act out because they have insecurities.

The higher your selfesteem and the more you feel like you accomplished in a day, the better you are going to be with the people around you; your spouse, your planner, your boss, your family, and friends. When you increase your positive self talk, you decrease your negative thoughts. And negative thoughts are toxic to your soul and your dreams.

I challenge you to monitor your thoughts for 24 hours. Keep track of how many destructive thoughts run through your brain. What ever the voice inside is telling you and what ever harmful thoughts appear, write them down. I would be very interested in seeing how many of these negative notions cycle through your thoughts. When one of them appears say, "No thank you...I choose not to believe it" and direct your frame of mind with "I am perfect with my imperfections." It is important to shape your thoughts and attitude in a way that empowers you; it is a beautiful way to be more loving and kind to yourself.

"Don't put off something that can be done today."

Mary Dann-McNamee

"All Is A Gift. It is up to you to find it in all you do."

Mary Dann-McNamee

Increase Your Knowledge

Another key aspect of being mentally balanced is in education. Whether you are going to school, taking classes, reading magazines or talking to professionals, it is most important that you fill your mind with the proper facts to be able to make the appropriate decisions. Being an informed planner for a wedding does take a lot of time to get up to speed with the tips, trends, ideas, and tools to manage certain vendors and aspects of the wedding planning process. If you do not want to spend your time doing the work and research then go to a professional who has already studied and been trained. A professional planner can guide a bride through the wedding planning process with less stress and more control.

Most brides find the planning process overwhelming and difficult at some point throughout the process. Planning a perfect day, staying in budget, and navigating all the decisions, can be much more difficult than they expect. If your strengths are not organization, creativity and managing stress, you may want to consider getting out of the planning role.

Spiritual Balance

Spiritual balance is making time to connect with your spirit and your higher power through actions, words and thoughts. Everyone practices their own walk with their soul and spiritual self. What's really important is that you take the time to discover it and build a relationship. Allowing your spirit to breath and glow is instrumental in cultivating a relationship with yourself. Whether it is taking a euphoric experience in nature or lighting a candle at a church, finding your place or space to connect with your higher power is imperative to being balanced and will allow you to center yourself in life.

What is your spiritual self? Is it nature? Is it God? Is it Jesus? Is it Love? Is it Light? Is it Buddha? Is it Zen? The main thing is that you do get connected to it because it is an essential piece to the four components of balance. Finding or being open to discovering a spiritual advisor can be rewarding and liberating. A spiritual advisor is someone you can open up to about your current and past beliefs. Someone who will help you choose your true beliefs and compassionately dispel old beliefs that may be conflicting to your true self.

Being Present

If I am present in the moment then I do not stress about the future because I am confident I'll know what to do when the time comes. I limit my toxic thoughts of "what ifs" and the "should've" "would've" and "could've". These blind me from seeing the gift of my present situation. I find that being present in the "now" equips me with assurance to know I can handle the future. Looking at your "list of things to do" can be overwhelming. I have experienced many brides and planners that are drowning in their work loads by allowing the pressure of "I should get it all done," to stifle them. My best advice has been to take small steps to chip away at your tasks and then recognize your accomplishments. Being the best at what you do means doing one thing at a time and accepting with a sense of peace that it will get done and that you can do it.

"You are perfect even with your imperfections."

Mary Dann-McNamee

Being Grateful

Gratitude is a choice and an acknowledgement of the gifts that surround me. I have created a habit in my life of being grateful. It is a powerful preference of thought that allows me to overlook painful or challenging situations in life. I am very grateful for my past as it is given me the gift of today.

Grace and appreciation for the moments throughout my day means counting my blessings for all that I have, all I have been, and creates room for all that I would like to be.

For a professional planner it is important that you feel obliged for the honor, and gift of a client's trust to move them through their journey towards the alter.

As a planner, the more gratitude I feel, the less frustrated I feel towards my clients. If I am thankful for the opportunity to be a part of my clients' experience, I am more joyful to handle their adjustments, dramas, differences and last minute changes.

As a bride, it is important to be grateful and thankful that you have found your soul mate and that you have chosen each other to be able to move through life's journey together. When it is all said and done whether there are two people at your wedding or one thousand, the priority is that you are coming together, heart to heart, to celebrate the union of your love.

Personally, I have had the experience of being a bride twice. I found it important to thank my spouse-to-be for the contributions he was making. I acknowledged what he was contributing rather then what he was not contributing. This made for a much more harmonious planning process. For brides, I offer you the opportunity to try it. When you focus on what you have, rather than what you do not have, your feelings of joy are more available.

For instance, when I think of all the things that I have rather than what I do not have, I feel abundant, and full. This practice helps me to judge myself less and be more caring to others. The brides that have the best time on their wedding day are the brides that practice gratitude as they plan and make it a lifestyle choice.

Finding the Gift in the Everyday

It is your job and your responsibility to be able to find the gift in everything that you do. Once you do find the gift, the stress seems to melt away. The things that meant so much that was not happening doesn't mean as much anymore. Usually, when you do find the gift and you are thankful, life gets better. You cannot have stress if you are having joy. You are not able to have anxiety and pressure if you are experiencing a gift. Being connected to your higher power will help you find that gift. It will allow you to get out your own mind and be able to see the bigger picture. Take a moment, a breath, a walk, a little time and just put a "pause" in your busy life. Now you can be grateful for the bigger picture, the family and friends around you, and the people in your life that love you. These are the important things that move you through life's challenges and difficulties.

"You are enough and you have enough, no matter what anyone says or does."

Mary Dann-McNamee

"We are all loved abundantly, no matter where you are born."

Mary Dann-McNamee

A Sacred Event

Whatever your religious practice is, the event and experience of wedding planning is sacred. It is not so much about the napkins, the favors, the lighting, the flowers, the furniture, the invitations; it is really more about the spiritual connection between two people and the celebration of their union and love. If you are a bride or a groom, make sure that you check in with your companion-to-be's thoughts and feelings throughout this process. Every time you feel nervous or stressed on that day for whatever reason that might come up: family, relatives, and the food, who knows-just remember the words "thank you". These are the most powerful words that you'll ever say to yourself and your higher power throughout your day.

Emotional Balance
Being emotionally balanced is connecting with my "child-self." It is more of my heart centered experience of the world. My emotional self empowers me greatly to be able to extend

myself in ways I never felt I could extend myself because my heart is in it. It is important that your emotional self is part of the planning process, whether you are the planner, or the bride. It is important that the planner dials into the bride's enthusiasm and excitement for certain things throughout the planning process.

I often see brides unsure on how their dream ideas will pan out or actually look on the wedding day. A good planner can always pick up on a bride's "sparkle in her eyes" as she describes a flower or detail about her dream wedding day. When I am open to a bride's "sparkle" I feel what she feels for that detail or idea. I help her tease out the idea and help her bring it to life. If may not be my personal preference but since it is a brides, I put myself in her shoes, tap into my past experiences and make it happen for her. Often times, better than she expected! Getting out of yourself and into the dream of your client is a gift and honor!

It is essential that the bride shares her ideas and excitement through various ways while she is working with a planner. If you are a planner or a bride, please get a professional that is excited, thankful and experienced to help pull off your wedding celebration. To implement the balance of being emotional while being a wedding planner is to be able to be excited with the bride to feel and understand what she is experiencing.

When I am working with a client and we are in a meeting and their eyes light up, that is a big cue to me. It is saying, "Oh boy, this is important. Staying emotionally connected to your bride without getting sucked into all the emotions or drama is vital. You must remain grounded and be sure that you are "dialed in" to what's emotionally going on with your client.

For brides, being emotionally balanced is to refrain from letting your emotions take over. It is to stay grounded enough in the other aspects of balance so that your emotions do not take the best of you. It is not only your day, it is your groom's day, and it is a day that allows your whole family to come together; a reunion with your favorite people, family, and friends. It is a beautiful experience and it is so much more beautiful when a bride is absolutely balanced, especially emotionally on her wedding day.

"What ever the question,

the answer is LOVE. *"*

Mary Dann-McNamee

Communicating Your Emotions

It is important that you check in with yourself to make sure that your feelings are being heard and understood. Are you sharing your feelings with the appropriate people at the appropriate time? If you are speaking out at inopportune times and you are not getting heard, you are only going to get more frustrated. Instead if you carve out the time to speak heart to heart with somebody when the issues are cropping up, it will allow you to curb the emotions that inhibit happiness and balance.

When you communicate from the heart, you set yourself up for success. It is important to create the time and space for your heart to speak. Whatever it needs to say; do so in a kind, compassionate way. Once you get out what you need to say, most often, your planning process will go along much more smoothly. If speaking from the heart is difficult, I recommend writing your feelings in a letter, editing as you feel necessary and reading it out loud to the intended person or persons.

I know how hard it is to have an idea of what you want to say and then when you get your intended audience, you cannot communicate as you had intended. So frustrating! I grew up in family that was very busy and hectic. There were time limitations and budget restriction with patience being a resource shortage. There were not many long conversations.

I was the fifth child in a family of six siblings, so as a young adult, when I had difficult decisions or feelings to communicate, I would usually write a letter and ask the intended audience to please hear me as I read my thoughts and feelings. I did it as a child, why not keep doing it? It gave me chance to be (usually) uninterrupted and to be fully open for my feelings and thoughts to be heard (rather than staying in my brain to play over and over). It was so liberating to finally get my full thought out rather than piece by piece.

Time for the Emotional Self

With the busy schedule I maintain, it has always been important for me to make time for my emotional-self to be free. This is where I usually get to be playful, unconventional, non-sensical, and just being in the moment with great joy. I make time to be emotionally balanced by allowing myself the break to let loose and do something that doesn't take a lot of thinking. It doesn't require a lot of effort or physical activity, but yet gives me the time to just have fun and play like a child. I enjoy drawing, writing in my journal, playing with my children (three and one year old), listening to music and nature.

My recommendation is to discover a hobby or re-connect with an old hobby. Keeping in mind a hobby is an activity or interest pursued outside one's regular occupation and engaged in primarily for pleasure. The hobby I am recommending is a hobby that one does not receive compensation. I LOVE 95%

of my tasks that I participate in as I create and execute special weddings and parties for my clients and only LIKE 5% of the tasks. It is easy to make your work your hobby when you are doing something you love. So it takes discipline to schedule time to "play" in order to exercise your hobby.

"Doing nothing is doing something."

Mary Dann-McNamee

Therapy

Another important tool to staying emotionally balanced is to enlist the help of a professional therapist. He or she should be somebody that you can share openly from your heart regarding your frustrations, sadness, anticipations, anxiousness, or whatever you are moved to share. It is an amazing experience to have someone that can be there for you with an open mind and heart. There are a fair share of people you can muster up to listen to you all day long, but do they hear you with an open mind and without casting judgment? Usually friends and family cannot give you a full hour of just you, without interrupting.

Over the years, I have instructed many professional planners, who have come to me for career counseling, to be open to the guidance of a therapist. This allows planners the opportunity to unload issues that are bothering them, where they are not being judged and can be seen objectively through a different perspective. On the same note, couples often explore the guidance of counseling through the wedding planning process because of issues that have creped up unexpectedly.

A bride and groom are often asked to do so much in such a short amount of time. When they do start their planning process, they are not only managing their plans and expectations, but those of their parents as well. This becomes a combination of the groom and his family traditions with those of the bride and her family's customs; all meshing together to make this spectacular experience remembered by everyone forever.

It is a lot of pressure; emotionally, there is going to be set of issues that present themselves. If you can talk to a professional, your heart will find a safe place to be for awhile. It is going to be most important to do this during the wedding process so that you keep your sanity and stay more balanced. You are human with a beautiful heart and you deserve the balance. It will happen; you just need to manage it when it does.

"*If you want the same results, continue to do the same behavior. If you want different results then act and chose differently. After all, insanity is doing the same thing over and over again, and expecting different results.*"

Mary Dann-McNamee

The Law of Attraction

When being emotionally balanced it is important to stay in tune with the law of attraction. By this I mean, what you create for yourself and within yourself is what you'll attract. So if you generate drama and chaos and are comfortable with it, you are going to be a magnet for more drama and chaos. There is no other way around it. How you treat yourself is what you are going to attract from other people around you. If you do want less anxiety in your life, be less stressful on yourself.

If you want less drama around you, allow less dramatic thoughts to move through your body. The words "always" and "never" are extreme words that are actually toxic to your well-being. The calmer you are and more balanced you are in your internal self then the more peace and balance you are going to attract in your life. As a planner, I can usually sense a bride with high drama when they come to meet with me. If they are considering hiring me, I will assess if she enjoys her flair for the dramatic. I personally would not be a good fit for a bride who likes high drama or is comfortable with lots of last minute details. I would not be one to throw more gasoline on the fire of controversy and drama. I am the one wanting to put out the fire, or certainly more over, recommend somebody else that would be a better wedding planner for them.

I have experienced some brides in my many years of wedding planning that like others to feel like they do not know what they are doing. Thankfully, I have had many more brides that enjoy organization, calm and following a stress-less path.

One of my favorite brides was a bride that was very detailed. She could articulate her needs, wants and wishes. Unfortunately, to most people's standards, she would be considered "picky" She was very eager to answer my questions. To most peoples standards, she might be considered obsessed with "wedding details" or be diagnosed Obsessive Compulsive. I found her to be very secure with herself in many aspects of her life (this is vital because, this personality type will usually be generous with their compliments and express gratitude for all you do).

My favorite brides/clients are usually an only child or the first girl getting married, upper middle class, in a close relationship with their family (especially their mother), usually in their late 20's and able to recognize and trust a professional. This type of client is one of my favorites because I feel most purposeful escorting them through the emotional and physical journey of planning a dream day; a day that has so much meaning and joy. It is an experience that will leave a lasting impression on all the hearts and minds that attend. I recommend making a list of your dream client...describe attributes and qualities. This will help you attract the perfect client for you.

A bride that was not a good fit, was one that seems to want to tell me how she hopes things or how she has seen something for less or more on the internet or has several friends who all want to help in her on her wedding day. I do not mind working with one or two non-professional friends of my client, but I tend to experience more stress working with friends of the brides. High stress would include a bride that does not return calls or emails. Managing so many details that all have to be perfectly executed is not for the weak in spirit or the frail in body and heart. When a bride does not respect your time or efforts, it is most difficult to surpass her expectations.

"You can attract more bees with honey than you can with sour cream..."

Jack Dankowski (my Dad!)

Journaling

Another way to stay emotionally balanced is to be able to journal or write about some of the experiences that come up through your rite of passage. By this I mean, if there are issues that are coming up and bothering you, slowing your mind down long enough to express this on paper will create a healing process. It is very important that you take time to explore the challenges that are bothering you. Sometimes writing about things can help you decipher the truth of the matter. It slows down your mind so you can listen to the internal gage inside you and express it. Once the words are on paper, it becomes more manageable to deal with. New thoughts and solutions can begin to percolate. For me, writing has usually helped clear up confusion and reduce stress.

Trigger Points of Being Out of Balance

Some of the trigger points to be aware of that will show imbalances are:

- Being ultra sensitive, easy to shed a tear
- Inability to listen and hear other's point of view; i.e. cutting them off before they finish communication their thoughts or views

- Feeling that everyone is out to get you or take something from you
- Acting cranky from lack of sleep
- Drinking excessively (worse yet, drinking while on prescription medication)
- Overeating or eating excessive amounts of fatty/comfort foods
- Complaining about others

When you are experiencing one or more of these trigger points you need to take a pause in the planning process. I know that when I am tired or hungry, I am not in the best state of mind to be planning; whether I'm helping somebody or planning something for myself. So it has become vital for me to get enough rest, eat a nourishing meal, and be in a relaxed state to be able to get started at work or complete a task at home.

"Be still and know that I am."

Psalm 46:10

"Do your best and let God do the rest."

Mary Dann-McNamee

Part II:
WEDDING WISDOM FOR THE PLANNER

Learning About the Quality Traits of a Great Wedding Planner

Some of the traits that a great wedding planner has are the ability to manage a lot of different items. Excelling at being a mediator, director, leader, and crafty like a seamstress, are just a few key elements to being the best planner you can be. I tell all the girls on my team, "You leave your ego at the door; you are absolutely there to serve." If you find that the client is at a space where they cannot make a decision, then help them out with that decision. That is what they pay us to do. I am hired to be their expert, their coach, their producer, their therapist, and their friend. It is a sacred dance of doing things for them that they may or may not acknowledge. It is helping them get the credit for the beautiful choices they make. It is letting their voice be heard. It is being excited for their vision, even though it may not be your personal choice.

If you participate in celebrations, whether it is birthdays, anniversaries, or graduations, you have the basic elements to become a wedding planner and help people through their rituals and through their celebrations. As a planner, I have often been asked, "Oh, what's the worst thing that ever happened? Oh, did a cake ever fall? Tell me a crazy story about a wedding-such as did a bride get scared and not show up?" So often, outsiders to our business are fascinated by the disasters. It is like an accident on the freeway, everyone wants to take a look. I can thankfully say I do not have tumultuous stories to tell and it may be because of the way I conduct myself and my perspective on things. If something doesn't go right at one of my events I do not look at them as a negative experiences, but I look at them as opportunities to grow. Some of the ways that I learned about protocol and etiquette for weddings is reading many books and magazines through the years that I worked in the hotel industry. I started reading as much as I could. It felt like I couldn't get enough. I was so excited to absorb everything and expand my knowledge. I wanted to know all the different cultures and what happen during their ceremonies. Finding out what's acceptable in one culture and what's not acceptable in another was so fascinating. Inspired by their color palates and rich customs and traditions I was able to understand more of their vision for a wedding. So it was very important for me to learn all the different nationalities and their various rituals for celebration.

It was very fun to learn all the different cultures and rituals because I am very interested in humans, their behaviors, and the mystique behind why they do what they do. I found that so many different cultures have really similar veins that run through all of them and it is so much about love, acceptance, commitment, and forgiveness. There are certain rituals that signify different things, but there are certain items that will be a common thread throughout every type of wedding celebration. What's so exciting for me with weddings rather corporate events or parties are I love the idea that all the emotions culminate on this one day. Weddings are the riskiest type of event for a planner to produce. Corporate planning can be so challenging, but there's nothing more precarious than navigating unchartered territory of an imagined perfect day.

"Do unto others as you want them to do unto you."

Matthew 7:12

How to Deal with Challenging Clients

Challenging clients or challenging brides, I look at it as they are giving me an opportunity to grow. They are asking my subconscious and conscious to expand my ability to be tolerant and compassionate. So nobody is impossible for me to work for or with. How I look at is, "Oh, OK now I have to raise my bar of compassion, tolerance, and kindness." The balance is being able to give to yourself and take care of your soul so that you can actually give to other people, while handling the hearts and souls of others during the short time that you are blessed by their presence.

Everyone's journey is different and it is up to me as a person on this earth to be able to honor everybody's journey at the pace they want to go. No wonder a bride can be so undecided, ungrateful and demanding; planning their wedding is like planning their own Academy Awards night. There are paparazzi, gowns, tuxedos, happy people, and a lot of excitement. The couple gets rewarded, is praised all day, and experiences their own sense of royalty. It is the only time that their friends and family are going to be around them and surrounding them all at the same time celebrating with them at moment like this. The next big inclusive celebration could be at another rite of passage...a funeral.

From my experience, I have developed several tips to dealing with challenging clients so that you can hopefully avoid conflict and create peace:

- ❖ Put yourself in their shoes and empathize with them. Let them know they are being heard. Sometimes people just want to vent and they do not need for you to fix anything. Just listening can be "fixing."
- ❖ Refrain from bragging about yourself or past clients. Keep your family life out of conversations with this type of bride. She is liable to think you do not care about her. Make sure it is about her, not you.
- ❖ Return her calls sooner than you return others. The longer you put off the return call, the more she is distorting her thoughts and becoming angry with you.
- ❖ "Kill her with kindness." Most people who are difficult and unstable have a long list of issues. It is obvious not enough people modeled kindness to them. Be a light in the midst of their little dark world. They act out because they are wounded. I have always felt that broken people do things to try and break others. Be strong in compassion, rooted in love and delight about forgiveness.
- ❖ Increase your ability to give them compliments (when and where they are due) in a genuine manner.
- ❖ Praise them and their choices. Random acts of kindness and compliments can go a long way. Even if they do not listen or believe it, it is a positive habit to acquire.

Lastly, it is (sometimes) ok to dissolve an agreement. If someone or the sum of people are too difficult to deal with and consistently discount you or your services it may be time to let go of the toxic relationship and "break up." A healthy dissolution would look like this:

1. Calculate the money they have invested in your services
2. Fairly evaluate the hours invested to service them. (By "fairly" I mean what you actually did and what they perceived you did. After all, someone's perception of you is their reality of you).
3. Research options for another planner for them. Maybe someone with flair for dysfunction or a novice planner that is open to be dictated to.
4. Create a kind and compassionate letter that starts off with thanking them for the opportunity to work with them this far. Then add something like "I am not feeling helpful or enough for you and your expectations... I have enclosed _____ and wish you well..."

If you are dissolving the relationship and you have not made a cancellation clause in the contract, do not plan on billing them for any outstanding monies. Move on and make room in your heart, mind and calendar for more beauty, love and joy.

I have never fired anyone, but if I needed to, I would do what I have instructed above.

I have, however, been told that my services were no longer needed. It has happened to me twice in the 18 years of business and 500+ wedding celebrations.

Once to an uppity Chicago mother and tomboy rugby player daughter who came to the planning table with many years of past hurts and pain towards each other. I found myself being the third party in their drama triangle. I prayed for clarity and what to do and asked for strength to carry out my commitments with a positive attitude. Thankfully the Lord released me from my commitment. I actually gave them back more money than they expected and I was happy and relieved to let it go.

The other dissolution of an agreement came when the mother of the bride "hired" me two months before the wedding. I was aware of the fact that the mother had unstable behaviors and even addictions, but did my best to be patient with them. Our professional relationship turned dysfunctional when she continuously showered me with praise, only to then cut off our contract via a chilly e-mail. In this instance, I really liked her daughter, the bride, but unfortunately her mother was paying for the wedding and was therefore very involved in the process. I was emotionally drained from the experience; however, as all things do, it worked out for the best, as I was able to take a family vacation on what would have been her wedding weekend and shortly after learned I was pregnant with my second daughter. Thankfully, when I no longer had the stress of that client in my life, I allowed more joy to come my way!

Warnings of a dysfunctional bride or mother-bride combination:
- ❖ Shops and meets more than three wedding planners
- ❖ Has fired at least one wedding planner already
- ❖ Self admits she can be a "bridezilla" or brings up out of the blue, "I am NOT a bridezilla."
- ❖ In the initial consultation she seems to talk more about how great she/we are at planning rather than asking about how you work

"Just when you think you have enough compassion and tolerance, another bride comes along and raises your bar for compassion and tolerance. Thank God."

Mary Dann-McNamee

Building a Foundation for Growing a Successful Wedding Business

Before your ideal dream wedding planning business can be realized it needs to be built on a sturdy, strong, but flexible foundation; a foundation that will stand the test of time.

Internally make sure you are feeling well, fulfilled, and confident. Make sure your heart is open with daily gratitude and a compassionate nature. You have to be open for the gifts of success to come your way. The gifts of prosperity and abundance cannot come your way until you are prepared, organized, and open to the possibilities.

Externally create systems to prepare and sustain a busy future load of inquiries, phone calls, and emails. The skeleton of my foundation are the forms and systems I have in place that help me build more opportunities to grow, thrive, and experience balance.

These forms are included for you here:

<u>Inquiry Sheet</u>

This sheet helps anyone assisting the office to extract the proper information from any potential client who is inquiring about my services.
Note: Always have plenty of blank spaces to add additional vital information like: colors they like, locations the have already seen, parents' info, what they do for a living, etc.

Mary Dann
WEDDING AND PARTY COORDINATORS

Today's Date: _____ Event: _____

Name (s):_____

Address: _____

Home: _____ Work: _____ Fax: _____

Cell: _____ Email: _____

Rehearsal: _____ Ceremony: _____

Event Date: _____ Location: _____

Bridal Party: _____ # of Guests: _____ Referral Source: _____

First Meeting: _____

Florist: _____

Photographer: _____ Video: _____

Ceremony: ___ _____ Officiant: _____

Cocktails: _____ Entertainment: _____ Dinner: _____

Other: _____

Tentative Client Folder

This folder holds all tentative (anyone who has not signed a contract or sent a deposit) until they decline our services or move to their own "definite file" folder. I recommend a different color of file folder so it is easy to find. Make sure you have blank inquiry sheets attached to the file as well. Accessibility is the key. I go through this folder every one to two weeks to check up on tentative clients and follow up on possible decisions that have been made. Once they decline or do not return my call, I remove them from my file and get rid of their paperwork for good. I used to save them thinking they may change their mind but it didn't seem to be useful, so I stopped.

Creating a Detailed, Yet User Friendly Contract

This agreement would be for a potential client who has not started the planning process and does not really know how they will need you. If the potential client doesn't know which package to choose, then you may want to first discuss her option and then verbally confirm the contract she will receive. I have provided an inclusive sample contract and my standard contract cover letter. Exact pricing is determined once you meet with a potential client. Please remember you can always drop your price to secure a contract, but you cannot ever go back and ask for a higher price later.

Wedding Coordination Contract

Bride: Groom:
Address: Address:

Phone: Phone:
Email: Email:
Wedding Date: Time:
Ceremony: Reception:
Location: Location:
Package: Package Fee:

Service Description
Name of Package

Maximum of Five (5) Consultation Meetings (Four (4) hours maximum per meeting):

Initial meeting to discuss vision, priorities, and budget, including creative brainstorming consultation in regards to décor, florals, stationery, linens, lighting, etc.

I really want to make sure I can "WOW!!" my clients, therefore an initial consultation is a time for them to get to know me and I have an opportunity to get to know them. I know I do my best work when I really like the people I am helping!

- Site inspection to potential location in _____
- One vendor meeting of your choice (we recommend the floral design)
- Attendance at the final catering detailing
- Detailed planning session to discuss wedding day itinerary and ceremony
- Final meeting 4-7 days prior to the event to finalize the wedding day itinerary and collect all wedding items to be set up by Mary Dann Wedding & Party Coordinators (guest book, cake servings set, toasting glasses, seating cards, place cards, table cards, favors, additional décor.)

Planning Services Provided Prior to the Event:
- Complete access by telephone and email to Mary Dann Wedding & Party Coordinators for any questions
- Evaluation by questionnaire of personality, preferences, and priorities
- Customized budget analysis
- Customized detailed planning checklist
- Customized overview planning checklist
- Personalized vendor recommendations to fit your

needs and preferences
- Assistance scheduling and arranging vendor appointments
- Assistance communicating with <u>ceremony sites</u> and <u>reception site</u>
- Available to review all vendor proposals and confirm services with contracted vendors
- Provision of customized itineraries for vendors, bridal party, and family
- Direction of wedding ceremony rehearsal

<u>Complete Wedding Day Coordination</u>:
- At least, two (2) wedding day assistants included
- Greeting and directing vendors at site
- Monitoring of set up
- Receiving deliveries
- Delivery and set up of wedding items that were provided by client at final meeting
- Limited set up of florals, linens, and other items per discretion of Mary Dann Wedding & Party Coordinators
- Close monitoring of schedule & itinerary
- Assistance with attire & florals (tying ties, pinning corsages & boutonnieres, busting gown)
- Coordination and cueing of ceremony (detailing the appearance, posture, & pacing)
- Direct reception events in tandem with master of ceremony
- Communication with catering to streamline menu delivery
- Guiding the client through the day keeping the bride, groom, and parents abreast of upcoming events (first dance, cake cutting, and other various details)
- Pack up any wedding items (extra favors, toasting glasses, other personal items)
- Transport gifts to vehicle

Contract Terms

AGREEMENT/CONSIDERATION In consideration of the performance of the above-listed services by Mary Dann Wedding & Party Coordinators, including any that are subsequently agreed to in any written addendum to this agreement. Client agrees to pay an initial non-refundable payment (_____ _____initials) of $_____ in a check, cashier's certified check, or money order in or before _____date_____ which represents 50% of the total projected cost of the services, and to pay the balance in the sum of $_____ not later than 7 days prior to the scheduled day of the event.

(OPTIONAL)
EVENT INSURANCE Client agrees to obtain a property damage and liability insurance policy at a minimum coverage of $1,000,000 for the day of the event. This may be done through wedsafe.com as a rider on a current homeowner's policy, or through another entirety. Mary Dann Wedding & Party Coordinators will provide, on request, referrals to at least 2 separate providers.

HOURLY SERVICES AND CONSULTANTS FEES Clients also agrees to pay Mary Dann Wedding & Party Coordinators which of when contracted "hourly services" not specified in this contract at the rate of $120 per hour, which sums shall be billed and due and payable within fifteen days of the date of the presentation of the statement or invoice. If Mary Dann Wedding & Party Coordinators arranges or supplies any services or products not specified in this agreement, a consulting fee of 15% shall be charged for such items. The final payment for any hourly services and/or fees provided shall be made within seventy-two hours of the event. In no event shall Mary Dann Wedding & Party Coordinators bill for hourly services or consulting fees unless agreed to by Client before such services are rendered. In the event that hourly services or consulting fees are required. Mary Dann Wedding & Party Coordinators shall provide an estimate of cost to Client before undertaking said services.

ADDITIONAL EXPENSES Client also agrees to pay Mary Dann Wedding & Party Coordinators for the actual costs of any expenses or costs not listed above or in the attachment, which shall be based on the presentation of a bill or invoice for such costs or services, and such items will be paid within fifteen days of the presentation of any bill or invoice for them.

CANCELLATION/LIQUIDATED DAMAGES In the event of cancellation of the event, Client is required to notify Mary Dann Wedding & Party Coordinators in writing as soon as possible. In the event of a cancellation by the Client more than 60 days prior to the event date, the deposit shall be treated as liquidated damages by the parties. In the event of cancellation by Client less than 60 days prior to the event date, the following cancellation charges will apply based on the cancellation date's relationship to the scheduled date of the event plus any additional expenses incurred:

> (1) Less than 6 months; 50% of the balance of payment shall be due at the time of the cancellation.
> (2) Less than 30 day; Forfeiture of 100% of the contracted price (_____ _____ initials)

RE-BOOKING if client changes the date of the event, Mary Dann Wedding & Party Coordinators will apply the non-refundable deposit to a new scheduled date for the event, subject to Mary Dann Wedding & Party Coordinators' services, which shall be based on the current pricing terms, and payment amount for that agreement.

UNKNOWN EVENT DATE If the date of the event is yet to be determined, indicated as "TBD" on the date of this agreement, Mary Dann Wedding & Party Coordinators reserves the right to cancel all services and return the deposit if unable to perform services on the date that is chosen.

VENDOR/SERVICE PROVIDERS Mary Dann Wedding & Party Coordinators will provide, upon request, a list of potential vendors or service providers to Client. Mary Dann Wedding & Party Coordinators does not expressly or impliedly assume any obligation or responsibility for the performance of or products provided by any sub-contractor or vendor for this event selected and contracted with by Client, including but not limited to , food or beverage caterers, ceremony or reception sites, entertainment, music, photographic or videographer services, hair or make-up design, production or décor services, rental items, wedding ceremony, floral design, religious service, supplies and favors, or event-site set up and configuration.

FORCE MAJEURE Parties agree that this agreement shall be subject to a limited condition of force majeure condition that will include an act of war, act of God, or act of nature that shall actually and significantly prevent the event from occurring on the scheduled date, but said force majeure condition is not intended to include ordinary events such as inclement weather, ill health of any person, or family disputes that might excuse any person's participation in the scheduled event.

INABILITY TO PERFORM The obligation of Mary Dann Wedding & Party Coordinators to perform shall be relieved in the event of riots, strikes, epidemics, acts of terror, acts of God, or any other legitimate condition beyond Mary Dann Wedding & Party Coordinators' control. Should Mary Dann Wedding & Party Coordinators be unable to perform her duties due, Mary Dann Wedding & Party Coordinators will diligently seek a qualified professional to perform her contracted duties.

IDEMNIFICATION Client agrees to defend, indemnify and hold harmless, Mary Dann Wedding & Party Coordinators, its agents, servants and employees, from any kind of demands, damages, or claims arising out of or occurring in the course of the performance of any of the obligations specified above, or providing any of the services related to the event, except those claims, damages or demands which are based on the sole and exclusive negligence or responsibility of Mary Dann Wedding & Party Coordinators, and its agents, servants, and employees.

RESOLUTION OF DISPUTES Mary Dann Wedding & Party Coordinators and Client agree in the case of any disputes arising out of or related to the contract or the performance of any of the services or obligations by either party related to the contract or this described event, the parties shall be resolved in the Superior Court of Los Angeles County, California.

BEST EFFORTS Mary Dann Wedding & Party Coordinators agrees to provide its best efforts to assist the Client in planning the event.

BREACH OF AGREEMENT In the event that Client shall withdraw from this agreement in favor of another wedding event coordinator or consultant, Mary Dann Coordinators shall be entitled to retain the deposit amounts specified above as liquidated damages. Client agrees to pay Mary Dann Wedding & Party Coordinators for all unreimbursed hourly services up to and including the date of the written notice by Client of their intent to pursue the event through another coordinator or consultant.

LOST, DAMAGE, OR STOLEN PROPERTY Mary Dann Wedding & Party Coordinators does not assume the liability or responsibility for any lost, stolen or damaged property of Client or any guests or attendees at any meetings, rehearsals, or the event.

RETURNED CHECK FEE There will be a $35 fee for any returned check.

LIQUOR LIABILITY Client understands that the laws of the State of California prohibit the furnishing of alcoholic beverages to any minor (under the age of 21), and that Mary Dann Wedding & Party Coordinators will assume no liability or responsibility for the conduct of any person or entity found to have furnished alcohol to any person or alcoholic beverages by any attendee at this event.

PROMOTIONAL CONSIDERATIONS Mary Dann Wedding & Party Coordinators reserves the right to obtain copies of photography and/or videography of the event for promotional or other purposes.

I hereby agree to all services set forth in this contract and agree to the terms and conditions stated. As a Client of Mary Dann Wedding & Party Coordinators, I agree to pay all the stated amounts in accordance with the terms specified on or before the dates specified.

Client's Name (Bride)
          Date

Client's Name (Groom)
          Date

Mary Dann-McNamee
          Date

Mary Dann Wedding & Party Coordinators
505 N, Sepulveda Blvd No. 11
Manhattan Beach, CA 90266
Phone: 310.372.4320
Fax: 310.3724524
Email: m@marydann.com
www.marydann.com

Room Block Request Form
This fax form makes it easier to communicate your request to
a potential hotel. It also shows them you are organized and
professional. Hotels are likely to give you a reduced rate when
you are professional and make their job easier.

Mary Dann
Wedding & Party Coordinators
"Your team of hospitality professionals…"
P:310-545-1827   Fax: 310.796.0854   E: m@marydann.com

Date:_____

To:_____

From: Mary Dann

RE: Group room block for _____Wedding

Thank you in advance for assisting me with the following
room block. I would greatly appreciate a competitive rate
(lowest available so that guests will not call-in and secure a
lower rate).

Date: _____

Thur	*Fri*	*Sat*	*Sun*
Guest rooms			c/o

Name: _____

Contact: Mary Dann, 310-545-1827

Reservation Method: Individual call in

Cut-off date: 30 day prior to arrival (_____), at
which time, any unused portion of the room
block will be released for general sell.

Location of the Wedding: _____

Thank you in advance for assisting me with the following room
block. I would greatly appreciate a competitive rate (lowest
available so that guests will not call-in and secure a lower rate).

Wedding Checklist for Bride & Groom

Thank you for allowing Mary Dann and team to assist in your vision for your very special day. The Wedding Checklist will help you stay on track while preparing for your special day. Please don't hesitate to call with any questions or concerns, 310-372-4320.

13 MONTHS,

- ❑ Mary to create a selected vendor referral list and send to Bride & Groom
- ❑ Mary to send you samples of bands & videographers
- ❑ Mary to send a detailed budget
- ❑ Plan engagement party (optional)
- ❑ Reserve and send deposit to Location
- ❑ Reserve and send deposit to Caterer
- ❑ Reserve and send deposit to Officiant

12 MONTHS,

- ❑ Choose your wedding party
- ❑ Collect pictures of flowers, cake design, bridal attire, room décor, etc.
- ❑ Organize a book or file to hold all your wedding details (a 3 ring binder works well)
- ❑ Choose your gown and veil (delivery takes 4 to 6 months; fittings and alterations can take 2 months beyond that)

10 MONTHS,

- ❑ Select your Save the Dates
- ❑ Meet and select your wedding photographer
- ❑ Meet and select your floral designer
- ❑ Meet and select wedding videographer
- ❑ Meet with and select lighting company
- ❑ Bride & Groom to register for wedding gifts (Bloomingdale's is great!)
- ❑ Secure your entertainment requirements, i.e. cocktail reception music, wedding reception music
- ❑ Start your guest list and have it typed
- ❑ Mary to secure group room blocks at various hotels for your guests (a

high, medium and low priced hotel)

8 MONTHS,

☐ Secure your wedding cake design with cake company
☐ Send out Save the Date notes/cards

7 MONTHS,

☐ Bride to select dresses for bridal party and the mothers
☐ Groom to select tuxedo attire for groom, groomsmen, ushers and fathers

6 MONTHS,

☐ Bride to interview hair and make-up and reserve preview appointment
☐ Secure a location and menu for the "fond farewell" brunch or continental breakfast (optional)
☐ Begin getting travel vaccinations if necessary

5 MONTHS,

☐ Order stationery i.e. announcements, invites, thank you cards, menus, etc.
☐ Bride & Groom to order wedding rings
☐ Bride & Groom to plan and book honeymoon
☐ Meet with your catering manager at Hotel to complete a food tasting and confirm your menu
☐ Book room for wedding night

3 MONTHS,

☐ Schedule rehearsal date and time
☐ Meet with Mary at Hotel to discuss design/décor. At the meeting we will:
    ☐ Discuss linens, lighting, tableware etc. with the designers
    ☐ View a sample arrangement from the floral designer
    ☐ Discuss site layout and floor plan
    ☐ Create your timeline
☐ Address and send out your wedding invitations (or Mary to help find a calligrapher who will do it for you) Take a complete invitation to have it weighed for correct postage beforehand
☐ Purchase bridal party gifts

❑ Meet with your entertainment for music selection (optional)
❑ Secure a location and menu for Rehearsal Dinner
❑ Purchase "going away" and honeymoon attire
❑ Order flower girl dress
❑ Collect information for newspaper or magazine announcements

2 MONTHS,

❑ Mary to arrange personal transportation for bridal party and family (optional)
❑ Mary to locate babysitting services, if needed
❑ Design and print wedding programs
❑ Design menus and coordinate place cards – have them printed
❑ Bride & Groom to complete engagement photo session with photographer (optional)
❑ Bride & Groom to write thank you cards as gifts are received
❑ Reserve a valet company (optional or if necessary)
❑ Check to make sure your passports are current, if necessary
❑ Choose favors

1 MONTH,

❑ Bride to schedule final dress fitting (wear shoes & lingerie)
❑ Confirm <u>Wedding Rehearsal</u> time and date
❑ Confirm <u>Rehearsal Dinner</u> and location
❑ Confirm Ceremony Music with musicians – Special songs, recessional, processional, first dance, etc.
❑ Receive final number of guests from response cards
❑ Complete floor plan of reception site
❑ Bride & Groom to decide seating arrangements for bridal party and family at ceremony and reception
❑ Obtain a marriage license (an be sure to check the expiration date)
❑ Plan out-of-town welcome gifts, optional
❑ Give photographer a finalized list of must-take pictures
❑ Do a trial run with hairstylist and make up artist (bring a photo of your dress)
❑ Meet with Officiant and choose readings for the ceremony
❑ Find/purchase: something old, something new, something borrowed, something blue

THREE WEEKS,

- ❑ Schedule a "spa day" for you and your bridal party (Optional)
- ❑ Send out reminder to wedding party regarding wedding attire, rehearsal times, etc.
- ❑ Purchase toasting glasses, cake knife and guest book (if you haven't received them as gifts)
- ❑ Confirm arrangement for out of town guests, by receiving a rooming list from selected hotels
- ❑ Review wedding day itinerary and make final changes
- ❑ Arrange guest assignments for each table
- ❑ Personally notify each outstanding response
- ❑ Complete wedding dress and accessory apparel
- ❑ Finalize guest list and reception seating
- ❑ Send out Rehearsal Dinner invites and Fond Farewell Brunch invites to all invited guests

TWO WEEKS,

- ❑ Retrieve a "rooming list" of your guests from the hotels for the delivery of hospitality baskets (Optional)
- ❑ Mary to confirm any changes with vendors and send them wedding day itineraries
- ❑ Bride & Groom to complete place cards and seating assignments
- ❑ Bride to pick up dress and break in shoes
- ❑ Confirm honeymoon travel and weather
- ❑ Schedule facial or other beauty treatments

ONE WEEK,

- ❑ Bride & Groom to pack for honeymoon
- ❑ Call in your final head count (to Mary or location?)
- ❑ Have place cards printed
- ❑ Take off work to enjoy family and friends

Completed Wedding Checklist

Just because the wedding is done, it does not mean the wedding planner is done… Closing out a client's file after the event is very important. I have attached a "Completed Wedding Checklist" for your review.

Completed Wedding Checklist

❑ Thank you letters w/ details of the event; make it personal!

❑ Tip receipts spent @ each event, usually between $100-$700

❑ Enter/update all vendor information from event into outlook or data base

❑ Break down the file (6 months after date), take out all extra papers and shred any credit card information

Sample Wedding Budget

Wedding Budget for _____ & _____			
May 10, 2008 - 150 guests			
Item	Quantity	Price	Total
PRINTED MATERIALS			
Programs	100	$5.00	$500.00
Place Cards	125	$1.50	$187.50
Menu Cards	175	$3.50	$612.50
Invitations, response cards & envelopes	125	$20.00	$2,500.00
Save the date cards & postage	100	$4.00	$400.00
Stamps & Stuffing		$275.00	$275.00
Guest Book (optional $300. Polaroid guest book)		$50.00	$50.00
Calligraphy of invites ($4. each), place cards ($1.-$2. each)		$600.00	$600.00
Welcome Note Cards	50	$4.00	$200.00
Subtotal			***$5,325.00***
BRIDE'S ATTIRE/BEAUTY			
Wedding Dress		$8,000.00	$8,000.00
Shoes, Lingerie, Hand Bag		$500.00	$500.00
Hair and Make-up for the Bride ($400.) &		$400.00	$400.00
Hair and make up for your bridal party:	5		$800.00
$75. for hair & $75. for make up			$0.00
Hair and Makeup for Mother of the Bride	1		$150.00
Subtotal			**$950.00**
CEREMONY			
Church musicians and soloist		$500.00	$500.00
(a guestimate)Church fee		$500.00	$500.00
Subtotal			**$1,000.00**

ENTERTAINMENT			
Cocktail reception			$500.00
9 Piece Band – Dinner-Dance			$7,000.00
Subtotal			**$7,500.00**
PHOTOGRAPHY AND VIDEOGRAPHY			
Photographer (2 shooters, 10hrs coverage, all proofs, engagement session, album and parents album)		$8,000.00	$8,000.00
Videography (1 full day)		$4,500.00	$4,500.00
Subtotal			**$12,500.00**
FLORAL DESIGN AND DECOR			
Florist			
Bride's bouquet	1	$200.00	$200.00
Bridesmaids bouquet	5	$80.00	$400.00
Boutonnieres & Corsages			$200.00
Ceremony (Aisle, Alter, Etc)			$1,000.00
Reception Centerpieces	20	$200.00	$4,000.00
Cake table		$200.00	$200.00
Additional misc. flowers for		$900.00	$900.00
ceremony and reception (place card table, sign in area, ladies rest room)			
Rentals			
Chairs	150	$10.00	$1,500.00
Linens, Design & Decor			
Fire-pit cocktail area & ballroom décor $1,000., custom linens $3,500., trees and hedges $800.			$3,500.00
Lighting			

Pin spots for dinner tables 20 @ $30., cake table $75., dance floor $250., ambience, etc.			$3,500.00
Subtotal			**$3,500.00**
Cocktail and Dinner RECEPTION			
Cocktail hour Hosted Deluxe Bar (3hrs)	150	$52.00	$7,800.00
Tray Passed Hors d'oeuvres (4@$5.57 per piece)	150	$23.00	$3,450.00
Wine with Dinner (estimate 2 glasses per person) 67 bottles @$35 per bottle	67	$35.00	$2,345.00
Champagne toast (1 glass per person)15 bottles @$35 per bottle	15	$35.00	$525.00
Plated dinner	150	$75.00	$11,250.00
Cake	150	$10.00	$1,500.00
22% Gratuity			$5,908.83
Site fee			$2,000.00
7.75% Sales Tax			$2,694.46
Estimated total for Venue Reception Charges			**$37,473.29**
MISC.			
Welcome Gift Bags for Guests	50	$20.00	$1,000.00
Ice Carvings	2	$650.00	$1,300.00
Base Plates	175	$6.50	$1,137.50
Wedding Coordinator and Staff (including overnight stays and per diem)		$10,000.00	$10,000.00
Subtotal			**$13,437.50**
GRAND TOTAL			**$81,685.79**

Standard Operating Procedures

A few key points from my SOP, Standard Operating Procedures, are included here. To assist with any new intern or assistant when they first start with my company are:

Handling Inquiry Calls
Write all notes on Inquiry Form
  A. Take down as much information as you can about the person, their wedding, their engagement, their style, the vendor info, what they are looking for/needing from a coordinator. Possible questions would be: what they do for work, what's their budget.

  B. Ask if they have been to Mary's website. If not, direct them to visit the site to view package options, pricing info, and also gallery of photos for ideas

  C. Tell inquirer Mary usually works with weddings where the budget is $600 - $1,000+ per person

  D. Tell inquirer that Mary will get back to them within 48 hours to chat with them further

  E. Leave inquiry sheet out in Mary's view so she knows to call inquirer

Booking a new event
  A. Upon return of a signed contract and deposit, make a copy of the signed contract. Mary must counter sign the copy of the signed contract. We send the counter signed contract to the client and we keep the original contract they signed. Also make a copy of the check and place the contract and the copy of the check into a new client folder on the left inside flap.

a. If an Event Manager is contracted to run the event: send the signed contract along with Mary's payment to the event manager

B. checklist, budget and vendor referrals should go out within 3 days

C. Video and music demos should go out within 7 days of signed contract and deposit

Emailing potential clients, current clients, vendors etc...
Always PRINT OUT communication that is relevant to the job or potential job.

A. Potential Clients inquiry as it will be added to their Inquiry Sheet and kept in the Tentative Clients folder so that we have necessary background info on client when speaking to them. Includes copy of contract that is sent out to them (once it is signed the potential client moves to a Permanent client file folder)

B. Any current client communication via email- must be printed out and placed in their file under the "communication" section of their file folder so we can refer back if needed

C. Vendor correspondence must be filed in the appropriate sections for each client, as it relates to respective wedding events & clients

Procedure for Client File Folders- (Label different sections below with mini post-its to separate various vendors)

A. Front Left Side - Info Sheet, Mary's contract, copy of the deposit check

B. Front Right Side - Budget, timeline, vendor referral list,

C. 2nd Left Side - Introductory meeting notes & diagrams & to do sheets

D. 2nd Right side - Emails and correspondence

E. 3rd left - Hotel/ Location site & room blocks

F. 3rd right - Vendor contracts labeled with mini post-its for: Photo/Video, Florist, Rentals, Lighting, Entertainment, Cake etc...

Moving an Event to a Three-Ring Folder
Usually do this approximately one month prior (if more than one event that month, do it six weeks out)
   A. Move all documents clipped to the outside of original file to the outside of the folder... this means work is still pending on those things.
   B. If you see a timeline on the front of the original folder you normally do not need to revise it unless Mary has instructed you to do so. You will make several changes to the original timeline throughout the process. You will have changes up to the very last week of the event, in which all revisions will need to be made at that point in time.

Typically do not need:
   ❑ Correspondence- most of this has already been addressed by the time of the wedding date so its not necessary to have in the new three ring folder
   ❑ Budget
   ❑ Referral list

Last 5 days of planning, the following need to be in folder:
   ❑ Seating list
        o Alphabetical order
        o By Table #
   ❑ Final timeline
   ❑ Final BEO
   ❑ Final diagrams

Event- Copies (Timeline, Diagrams, Guest Lists)
   A. Single-sided copies of:
        - Diagrams
        - Guest List version A-Z

> - Guest List version by table #

B. Long version timeline for event staff printed double-sided.
> - Copies to be given out on the day
C. Short version timeline for wedding party and those attending rehearsal
> - double-sided and no more than two sheets

Note: count total number of people that will be present at the rehearsal. This will give you the total number of copies to hand out at the rehearsal.

The shortened version should only have the details that the wedding party/family needs to know. (i.e. rehearsal information, rehearsal dinner/lunch location, hair and makeup schedule, photography schedule, transportation details, ceremony order and timing of cocktails and dinner)

Do it right the first time so it doesn't have to be re-done and have backup of your work, just in case an emergency happens and someone needs to pick up your file and complete the job.

How to Attract the High End Brides and Vendors

"Pretty, happy, organized planners with experience, substance and grace attract pretty-happy brides with high budgets." – Mary Dann McNamee

1) The best way to attract a better bride is to be better with your choices of whom you associate with while working and playing. I believe in the old saying "birds of a feather, flock together." Choose to be friendly with vendors that share your same core values. For me, that means they have integrity, grace, and style. Select people in your life to contribute to your dreams and goals, while avoiding people that are negative in thought and action.

2) Think of ways to "wow" your client. Be of service to them in ways that they may not expect. One of the ways I like to do this is not even before the wedding, but after, because leaving a lasting impression is not only special for your client, but can also lead to referrals down the road. To do that, I decorate the bridal suite with flowers (usually reused from ceremony area), scented candles (Votivo and Seda France are my favorite), draw a hot bubble bath (make sure it is extra hot, because it will automatically cool down for the couple when they finally arrive) and leave a wonderful note of gratitude for the opportunity to serve them.

3) Work smarter, not harder. As you work, think of ways to streamline your activities. For instance, if I walk up to put something away and I see something else that needs to be put away; I'll pick it up and put both things away. If I am assembling cards or programs, I'll do one step of the task at a time. If I am thinking of details for a wedding, I'll get the details to the right destination, rather than writing it on a sticky note and leaving it to be transferred to the right place at another time. Working smarter, not harder is synonymous to less procrastination!

4) Increase your self-esteem. Studies have shown that when you become more confident, others around you will sense that, including potential clients and they will be more attracted to you. If you lack self-esteem in the areas of style, organization and intelligence the better bride will sense that and not have confidence in your abilities.

5) Create opportunities to show support to high-end locations and catering managers.

If I have a client that doesn't have a venue and could be interested in a high-end location, I will meet with them in the lobby to discuss their wedding plans, visions, needs, and make time to stop by the catering office to drop off my cards, marketing materials, and a little treat. Call them first to say, "I am in your area and want to do a walk through of your lovely hotel and pick up a packet of information. I also have a little something I'd like to give you. When would be a good time to come by?" They'll remember your kindness and thoughtfulness and the more you have your name and face around a high-end venue, the higher your chances are of them referring a bride to you.

Create opportunities to interface with high-end hotels. In the beginning of my career, I would offer a potential bride complimentary assistance in calling around to various hotels/venues to check availability. It is important to offer the bride (no matter the package they have selected) your assistance with calling potential venues to check space and availability on their behalf. You are reminding venues that you like their locations (so they keep you in mind for future brides) and you are also achieving rule number two of "wowing" a potential bride.

6) Create interest in yourself. Submit an article to be published in a magazine that is interested in you paying for an ad. Ask to reduce the cost of the ad or try to avoid just placing an ad, and negotiate an article that you are passionate about to run in the same magazine as your ad. The editorial content that brides read is even more influential than an ad they see, but if you can do both, it just maximizes your impact on them.

7) Make the best first impression- remember, you only have one chance to do that! Make sure you are stylized, coordinated, and your nails are done! These may seem like small things, but in our business attention to detail is so important and its crucial you show you are able to do it.

8) Conduct strong follow through. Call back any vendor or client within 24 hours. If you cannot do so, then communicate in another way to let them know when you can get back to them, such as through an email or text message. Let them know you received their message and you will get back to them within a given timeframe. When you say you will do it, DO IT and hopefully sooner than they expect! Just because you receive an email or call after you've left the office, doesn't mean you have to call back or write back right away. Give yourself space to work on the best reply or solution, but still do so within a timely manner.

"We are all wealthy and rich, some just have more financial abundance than others."

Mary Dann-McNamee

How to Customize Your Wedding Package and Book the Best Bride

The sales process starts on your first conversation. This is when you will discover how interested you are in their wedding and gauge how interested they are in booking you. The initial meeting has three key parts that each contain important factors in making sure you book the best bride.

Getting started:
- ❖ How fast do you call back? You should get in touch with a potential bride within the first 24 hours of her contacting you.
- ❖ How pleasant do you sound in your tone? If you do not seem positive and enthusiastic in your tone, a bride will not feel like you are excited about her. Conversely, if a bride's tone seems off-putting because it is arrogant, negative, or otherwise distasteful, you should recognize that as a red flag.

Describing yourself and your services:
- ❖ Don't be afraid to brag a little. Rarely is client name-dropping ideal, but venue dropping and reputable vendor name-dropping can create more interest in your services as you introduce yourself.

❖ Avoid discussing exact monetary terms. Use ranges instead of being pressured into a price. Remember you can always go down in price, but you cannot always go back and ask for more money.

❖ Selling the service of wedding planning is selling a vision, a concept or dream, and they are buying trust. It is important to uncover their needs and expand on how your features will benefit them.

❖ When you ask questions, listen to their answers and take notes. Show the potential client you care and you like them.

Closing techniques and questions:

Once you have enough information from them you can now explain how you can help them. When you can give examples of how you can help them, it is time to close the deal.

Show enthusiasm and desire to have the honor and pleasure to assist them:

"I would love to be your planner. I have so enjoyed our time discussing your ideas. Working with you to create your dream wedding day would be an honor for me."

Outline clearly what the next steps will be:

"My next final step is to create a contract that goes through the various options we discussed today. I will get it to you by (specify date) and will give you one week to decide by signing and faxing back the agreement with a 50% deposit. The remaining balance will be due seven days prior to your wedding date."

Ask them their feelings:

"Does that sound like a realistic plan for you?"

"Have I covered all of your questions?"

"Is this meeting with me what you expected?"

"If you had to make a decision today, would I have the honor to be your wedding planner?"

In addition, explain what your next action step is once the contract is signed and received. For me, it is putting together a budget with a checklist and selected vendor referrals.

"The only thing you can count on is change."

Mary Dann-McNamee

Increasing Your Income Once You Are Established

This layer is about finding ways to help others and get paid for it. Develop ways to create a "win-win" situation for yourself and others around you. Challenge yourself to think outside the box.

Here are several options I have developed for my own business:

1. Choose your office space carefully.
The location of your office space can be a very important marketing and even referral tool. My office space increases my visibility for potential brides as it is next door to a bridal resource showroom, A Legendary Affair. I have been a vendor and have placed hundreds of stationery orders with Cynthia Adkins (owner of A Legendary Affair). Her business augments my business by having over 30 stationery vendors, and fifty wedding related products, such as bridal pillows, unity candles, favor ideas, etc.

I have subcontracted my office space to several professional vendors I respect and admire. The two photographers I have selected have pulled together their resources to invest in coordinating frames and photos on several walls of my office. They pay a portion of the rent; receive a key to meet with potential and existing clients (for which they call me in advance to schedule their meetings, just so we do not have conflicting appointments). They also showcase their photo albums and business cards for all to see when they come in to meet with me. They are also my first two referrals (not my only referral, but my first two) to any potential bride.

Some of my favorite vendors to share office space with are: custom stationery, flowers, bridal gowns, entertainments broker, photographers and videographers. Pulling resources together is risky but rewarding. If you have "like minded professional vendors" then it is a bonus!

"There are no problems, just challenges to grow from and opportunities to learn from."

Mary Dann McNamee

2.Listen to opportunity when it comes knocking.

In 2003, I was approached to be included in a new reality cable TV show, "Whose Wedding Is It Anyway?" which was a show that focused on the life of a wedding planner. I didn't know what to expect with the show, but thought it was worth giving a try. The crew would follow me to my meetings, weddings, rehearsals, out with friends, my family celebrations, yoga class, everything. This was the first type of show that actually focused on the planner and not the couple or bride. It did wonders for my business because people finally got a bird's eye view of what a planner does behind the scenes. I received hundreds of emails from individuals wanting to know how I got started, what classes in school I took, etc. I wanted to reply to all, but I just couldn't without sacrificing my current balance of family and work. So I consulted with Doug Brannigan from Envision Productions and produced my first DVD, *"The Path of the Wedding Planner."* The DVD was a great success and has sold over one thousand copies world-wide.

Since then, I have been featured on more than eight episodes of "Whose Wedding Is It Anyway?," as well as other shows.

I am thankful I took a chance and trusted the producers of TRUE Entertainment to capture the integrity of the bride and the planner.

In 2001, I was asked to help a friend (Tim Clegg, President of Americhip, Inc.) by accepting his niece for a three-week summer senior year internship. The high school intern was so excited everyday for being a part of my business and I realized there was another avenue for expanding my business through mentorship. Now, many years later, I usually have five to ten mentorship clients a year and find great reward in helping them along their path.

In 2004, I found more people needing direction in the wedding business and career choices. They were not sure what aspect of planning they really wanted so I began career counseling, via phone, or in person. It is an opportunity for individuals in transition or at a stand-still in their business to consult with me in a confidential, therapeutic setting and ask whatever they would like about the business. I open myself up to helping them grow professionally and healing whatever may be standing in the way of their progress.

In 2007, I received more emails from people wanting more information on planning and at the same time I saw a great need for "balance" in the wedding business. Planners and brides were spending more time worrying than enjoying the planning process, which led to the inspiration for my second DVD, *"The Balanced Planner"* I collaborated with James Reid of Manifest Videography to focus on achieving spiritual, mental, physical and emotional balance as one plans for their big wedding day and the DVD has been enthusiastically embraced in the industry.

3.Create additional services that people need.

Applying other creative talents or skills you have can be a valuable revenue source for your business. One of the best ways to do that in this industry is to learn or improve upon your calligraphy skills. I have chosen to focus my attention on other avenues of expanding my business as previously described, but if I did do calligraphy, I have estimated that I would increase my revenue by $5,000 a year. Not a bad bonus to consider!

4.Create a new product.

In 2007, I filmed an episode on WE television network's, "Platinum Weddings" which showcased an idea I created for a bride that could not use any type of rice, petals, bubbles, or dove release as she exited the church, but they really wanted fan fare! So I created the Wedding Wand- a festive wand adorned with colorful flowing ribbons that can be waved to celebrate the couple. Those unique products bring in additional calls and revenue to my company. I have sold over 20,000 wands since 2007.

In addition, in 2007, I finally got tired of writing individual thank you notes to all of my clients after the wedding or as a means to give my vendors their final payments before the wedding day. I could never find the right thank you note that conveyed my appreciation to a vendor for all their hard work or a cute note that a bride could send to someone in their wedding party. So I teamed up with Mimio, The Artistry of Paper in Pasadena, California, to launch a luxury gratitude note card line. It is dedicated to the business of weddings: thanking vendors for their services, thanking clients for hiring their planner, notes to ask a friend to be in the wedding, etc. We are in the midst of our second edition of customized luxury gratitude notes, due in 2010.

5. Diversify your wedding business.
Whether you are just starting out or you are a seasoned professional, thinking outside your comfort zone is necessary to maintain profitability in our ever-changing wedding business. You know you have the skills, so why not find as many ways to use them! And if and when times are slower, diversifying your skills will get you through. Some of my suggestions for using your skills to their maximum potential would be:

- ❖ Showcase your talents of party planning (not just weddings)
- ❖ Assist other professional wedding planners on the "day

of" if you are available

❖ Approach your church or temple to be a religious wedding planner

❖ Work with a high-end caterer in your area to be an onsite part-time party manager

❖ Work part-time in a bridal salon

❖ Open a bridal resource showroom

❖ Work part-time at a luxury hotel in the catering department

❖ Assist a florist or photographer in their studio

"There, before the Grace of God go I."

unknown author

Part III: WEDDING WISDOM FOR THE BRIDE AND THE PLANNER

Creating a Detailed and Organized Timeline Script for the Wedding.

My clients come in to do a timeline meeting with me usually two to three months ahead of time and we create a script for the weekend. It is a two to three hour meeting where I cover all the bases for their whole weekend. We discuss guest logistics and timing, including when will people be coming in from the airport, the rehearsal and rehearsal dinner plans, what time we will do toasts and family pictures at the wedding, the cake cutting, and all the other key elements that need to happen throughout that whole weekend. I also address their personal needs and go over what they are going to do to take care of themselves that weekend, how they're going to get their hair done, where are they going to get it done, where the spa is, and how are they going to find some time to relax and enjoy themselves. This is something they often haven't even thought about and it is so important.

Even some of my most professional and upbeat "all-star" brides lose it. They just do. There is something that they never count on and that is the emotional piece to this whole puzzle. They do not count on the feelings that get out of control, because guess what? They do. They are getting married. They can plan all they want but when it leads up to their day-the month out, and even the few weeks before, they get overwhelmed and it is natural because we are all human. I find that most of my clients have been in the event industry themselves. They are directors of catering, event planners, lawyers, people in very high power positions and yet they still want somebody that operates at the same level as they do, who will take them through the most special day of their lives in a calm, peaceful, creative, and playful way so they can enjoy themselves. Several times I have had situations during these timeline meetings where it actually becomes a therapy session. As a therapist, I find my mediation skills and my ability to assess situations quickly can help find a prompt solution or choice of remedies.

When creating an inclusive timeline it is important to ask the couple about their dream for the day, their perfect scenario, etc. Let them imagine with you. Give them choices and if they seemed to be overwhelmed, guide them to a selection.

I usually allocate at least two and a half hours for a healthy, balanced timeline with both the bride and the groom. I would discourage other family members from attending. I really want to connect with the bride and groom. Other family members can be a distraction and may bring their own agenda to the table.

One time, my bride and groom came into see me for our two-three hour meeting to layout their dream wedding day and shortly after we got started the bride admitted that she was pregnant with the groom's baby and she did not want to be pregnant on her wedding day. This was primarily because she wanted to celebrate (party like a rock star) with her slender figure. I gingerly tip toed around the subject, found out what the groom wanted and teased out what the bride wanted. Then invited them to take a look at what they might be feeling months after the wedding, or when their first born arrives. I wanted them to see past their wedding day and sample what they might feel like five, ten, twenty-five, years down the line. I also explained what studies tell us about how men and women grieve and cope with abortions. I also made it comfortable for the groom to share his feelings and he did not want to loose the baby. Clearly the bride was too wrapped up in the perfect day and she overlooked the miracle inside her and her loving groom's feelings. Eight years later they have two other babies, making it a family of five and from time to time hear about their updates, which usually include a "thank you for that special planning day, the day we decided to start our family!" It is memories I have like this, which remind me of what I have been called to do and how blessed I am to do what I love.

Here is a sample of what a Christian or Non-denominational wedding timeline would look like this:

In honor of

Bride and Groom

CEREMONY LOCATION: _____

RECEPTION LOCATION: _____

Rehearsal day (1 Or 2 days prior to wedding day)

> *4:30p: Mary to meet bride to receive the following: (30 minutes prior to rehearsal)*

- *programs (with ushers and on greeting table)*
- *bubbles (on each seat at ceremony)*
- *disposable cameras (1 one each table at reception)*
- *marriage license(with a check for $ 26. to receive 2 certified copies & self addressed stamped envelope)*
- *cd (first dance & family dance)*
- *guest book & pen (at the greeting table)*
- *place cards (to be set out during ceremony on greeting table or foyer of Restaurant Terrace)*
- *seating chart for dinner dance (a thru z and table # 1 thru # 17)*

5:00p: Wedding party and family arrives in Lobby for Rehearsal. Please list people in attendance:

5:10p: Wedding party and family proceeds to hotel's garden area for rehearsal review: walk thru procession, recession, cards, seating, panoramic photo, etc.

6:15p: Wedding rehearsal concludes

7:30p: Rehearsal dinner location (address and number)

Wedding Day

AM please list all the things you would to do in the morning, maybe a message or breakfast in bed??)

11:00a: Bride arrives to hotel to check into Bride's changing room, room#_____

11:45a: Hair and make-up stylist arrives to Bride's changing room, room# _____

12:00a: Note: Bridesmaids hair &make-up will take 20-30 minutes for hair and 20-30 minutes for make-up. Bride takes 2 hours for hair and make up)

Hair and make up schedule:

	Hair	Make up
12:	#1	#2
12:30	# 2	#1
1:	Bride	#3
1:30		#4
2:00	# 3	Bride
2:30p	#4	
3:00p:	All hair & make up done	

2:00p: Florist arrives to decorate the garden area
2:30p: Photographer, arrives in bridal dressing room to take shots of Bride, & her bridesmaids
                Note: all personal items must be cleared from guest room when all depart for photos
3:00p   Bride gets into her dress

                Florist arrives with personal flowers (male & female) to bridal dressing room

3:30p: Bride and Groom see each other for the first time (garden area)

4:00p: Wedding party meets in the garden for photographs

The following should be in
attendance:_____

5:00p: Family photographs.

The following should be in attendance (please list a
family remember to be responsible for making sure all
        family is in attendance- this is key, since a planner
does not usually know the invited family members)

5:30p: All photographs conclude
        Videographer arrives in garden area (or sometimes the
        videographer arrives when the photographer arrives)

5:45p: String duo arrives to set-up in garden area.

6:00p: Bridesmaids go back to bridal dressing room
        Groomsmen greet guests as they enter, pass out
        programs
        Encourage guests to proceed down the stairs to the
garden area

6:15p: Ceremony music starts to play in garden.

6:20p: Bride and bridesmaids go back to bridal dressing room
        Groom and Best man, Rabbi and Cantor stay in
        Director's room
        Family proceeds to the veranda doors to continue to
        greet guests

6:30p: Family and wedding party starts to line up for
procession

6:45p: Procession begins
        Song:_____
        Grandparents escorted by: _____
        Parents escorted by? _____
        Officiant:
        Groomsmen:

Best man:
Bridesmaids:
Maid of honor:
Ring bearer & Flower girl:
Music changes. Song: _____

Bride escorted by whom:

7:00p: Band arrives to set up in dinner room

7:15p: Conclusion of ceremony
        <u>Recessional</u> & group photographs. Please list all those
present

7:30p: Wedding photographs could conclude or go the full
        hour. If most photos are done before the ceremony
        then photos after the ceremony are usually 15-30
        minutes maximum.

        Bride and groom to proceed to a location for a private
15 minute reception and freshen up

        Rest of wedding party proceed to cocktail reception on
veranda

8:15p: Guests are asked to proceed to Dinner Reception
        Band starts
        Ceremony flowers & (5) cocktail arrangements are
moved to Dinner cocktail area

8:25p: Grand entrance (Bride and groom usually are
        announced & proceed to dance floor)
        1st dance. Song:_____
        Sometimes there is another song or two to get
everyone dancing and circulating

8:45p: Toast by parents of the bride and groom or host of the
        wedding

8:50p: Welcome prayer (optional)

8:55p: First course is served (each course is 25 minutes per course)

9:15p: Toast by best man & Maid/matron of honor

9:20p: Entrée is served (Bride and Groom to walk the room and greet guests)

9:45p: Father-daughter dance. (Usually the first song to open the dance floor right after dinner)
½   Bride and father of the bride
½   Groom and his mom
Parents and wedding party

10:15p: Dessert is served

11:45p: Cake cutting
Bride and groom toast
Bouquet or garter toss

1:00a: Conclusion of event
Who receives all the extra items at the end of the evening, such as:
- cake top
- extra programs
- gifts

Vendor information

(make sure the name, email, all phone numbers, start time and end time)

Name Company   Phone #'s   Arrival time Location
Mary Dann, Wedding & Party Coordinators
Office: 310.545.1827 Fax: 310.796.0854   E: m@marydann.com

Insights on Selecting the Right Vendors

Even when it comes time to choosing vendors or recommending vendors to my clients, for me it is about the value. I want to know several choices to help my clients find the best fit for them. I have always felt it is one of my jobs, as the coordinator to know high-end, low-end, and medium-end vendors in each category of vendors. So for me it is very important to have experienced my vendors before I refer them to my client(s). I do not want them to waste anytime because to me, time is money. I want to connect my clients with people that will fit their vision, their budget, and their personality.

If a vendor is late, difficult to deal with, or unprofessional, then I am less likely to use them again or refer them to others. Although I am open to working with new vendors, I prefer to work with vendors I have worked with because I can guarantee the work and service standards of my referral. I am most interested in the solution. So, I say take the time, give a pause, and start thinking about a solution rather than accentuating or putting more weight onto the problem and complaining about it. I really have vowed to make life easier for everybody I work with; the catering managers, my vendors, everybody that is part of the planning process and the execution of the wedding day for my clients.

At the weddings I plan, the bride and groom certainly are my clients, while their guests are also my clients, the bellman is my client, and the front desk agent is my client. Everybody that I interact with I treat as a client because it makes them feel valued and in turn, they are more inclined to offer their best service. I like choosing professionals that I can allocate to do different things in my life.

When it comes to cleaning my house I have a house keeper. Even though I enjoy cleaning, it is not the best use of my valuable time. To have my car cleaned and polished, I take it to a carwash. Time is valuable, so it is very important that you do not do too much in the short amount of time you are given throughout the day because overdoing your schedule isn't very fun and can be draining. You have to take into consideration what is the most valuable task to do right now. Even when it comes time to choosing vendors or recommending vendors to my clients, I consider the overall value.

Adopt An Attitude of Gratitude

I can usually tell when a bride is grateful for her family, friends, and vendors… she has a certain glow about her and is relaxed enough to enjoy her day to the fullest. She has let go of the differences and disagreements she may have encountered with all those involved, and rejoices in the true meaning of the day: a commitment to her mate. A grateful bride sees the day as a gift and avoids thinking of what she would have had, could have had, or should have had. And while it is important to feel thankful internally, it is just as important to share your gratitude with those who made your day so special.

Thanking Vendors

Vendors are the backbone of a successful event. The wedding industry may be a billion dollar business, but it is spread out over millions of small business owners who do what they do because they enjoy lending their talents and creating meaningful celebrations for others. It takes a unique sense of creativity, patience, and professionalism to thrive in this industry. Giving your vendors each a handwritten note of thanks for all they have done is a wonderful way to acknowledge the impact they have made on your day and your lives. Monetary tips are happily accepted, but a sincere note of thanks can often be the best way to show your gratitude for your vendors' hard work. Another way to thank your vendors is to print a few words of appreciation for their services in your wedding program or menu. Discretely including words of praise in this manner often works best for those vendors who will be present at your celebration, such as your photographer, entertainers, caterer, etc. It will allow them to enjoy your words of thanks while continuing to execute their part of the event.

Thanking Guests

Your guests increase the positive energy at your celebration, and thanking them for attending your event if they have traveled a long distance, is a thoughtful gesture. When it comes to giving favors as tokens of thanks, many couples will agree that they either want to do something beautiful and distinctive or nothing at all. If making the investment in traditional wedding favors is something you are considering, think about instead putting the money toward a charitable gift. A donation to a meaningful organization on your guests' behalf is a special and useful way to show your gratitude. Just make sure your guests are aware of the honor by placing a small card describing the charitable organization at each place setting.

If the traditional route is more your style, go the extra mile and personalize your favors. For example, you might request that your guests share their two favorite candies with you on the response cards. Once your guests take their assigned seats at the reception, their favorite candy will be waiting. Another way to show your gratitude is to have your valet service place a bottle of water and/or a single rose in each guest's car at the end of the night, with a thank-you note for a wonderful evening.

If you want to forego favors altogether, consider a touch that a recent client of mine incorporated into her celebration: the cake design included the names of each guest who attended the wedding. The designer monochromatically scripted each name in butter cream and all the names, swirled one after the other, made an extraordinary statement!

A low-cost idea that is sure to keep your guests feeling appreciated is including a handwritten thank you note on the back of each guest's escort card (the card that displays the guest's name and table number). The cards can even be sealed in miniature envelopes, providing a wonderful alternative to the common fold-over card. When one of my clients did this for her guests, I was thrilled to see how the note added a refreshing and touching surprise.

For the affluent, sophisticated and creative bride, a cutting edge favor idea is a custom video book or card. You can upload an edited video montage from your wedding celebration while your party is still going on. Then give the card or book out to each guest/couple as they depart your wedding day celebration. For more information, please visit my website, marydann.com or see www.artefactstudio.com

Thanking Your Wedding Party

Once you have selected the individuals that will make up your wedding party, consider sending them all handwritten notes of thanks for their roles of support. Once the wedding day arrives, presenting them with an additional gift is often appropriate to thank them for all they have done for you during your engagement and on your wedding day.

Personalizing these gifts is a wonderful way to ensure that your gratitude is properly communicated, and the recipient will surely notice your thoughtfulness. For your bridesmaids, think about filling monogrammed tote bags with smaller personalized gifts, such as semi-precious jewelry or a pendant with their first initial, an evening bag in their favorite color, a certificate for a spa treatment in their hometown, or any special memento that says, "This is just for you!"

As for the groomsmen, a monogrammed Dopp kit stocked with fine toiletries, a pair of personalized cuff links — either with their initials or a symbol of their home city — a tie that they can wear again after the wedding or tickets to their favorite sporting event or amusement park will go a long way to convey your thanks. One of my favorite wedding party gifts that are suitable for both men and women is personalized stationery. This gift not only shows your gratitude, but also helps continue the flow of gratitude to others in their lives.

Preparing for your wedding day is a time of grand decision-making wrapped up in a journey of much excitement. Remember to include "show gratitude" in your checklist of things to do so that your appreciation of all those who contributed to the experience does not go overlooked.

Conclusion

Now that you have tools to plan for your perfect wedding planning experience, insights on how I have done it, forms to help you stay organized and confidence to be your best as you plan for yourself or others, I wish you many moments of joy and gratitude and that you always remember to trust in your higher power. Above all, whether in life or business, the best rule to follow is my take on the Golden Rule: treat others BETTER than the way you have been treated! It will come back to you in beautiful ways.

In closing, I want to share some of my "Mary-isms." These little gems are the thoughts that inspire me and encompass my unique approach:

A hazard to being a successful wedding planner is that you will not have enough time to stay in touch with all of the many wonderful families you get to help along the way. Do not feel guilty about that, rather look back on each with fondness. I think of each and every family I have worked with (I have several large filing cabinets, housing wedding clients as far back as 1993) in a very special way. They all mean a great deal to me!

Birthing a "wedding day" feels somewhat similar to birthing a baby. It is very personal, very special and very exciting!

You are perfect with your imperfections!

Doing nothing in silence is doing something!

There are no mistakes, just lessons to be learned! All is in Divine order.

Whoever is supposed to be there, will be there.

Do your best and let God take care of the rest!

May you continue to feed your soul and create your OWN mantra to live an abundant life!

ABOUT THE AUTHORS:

Leila Khalil, Wedding Publicist (Co-Author)

Combining her personal love for weddings and her professional expertise in media and marketing, Leila Khalil created Be Inspired PR in 2007; a full-service public relations agency dedicated to giving wedding planners and vendors their deserved place in the spotlight. After several years of working as a wedding planner with many of the biggest vendors in the industry and achieving publicity for them in highly sought-after bridal publications and television programs, Leila officially expanded her services into strategic public relations and marketing consultation for clients in the wedding industry through Be Inspired PR.

As a business school graduate from Santa Clara University, Leila's career began in publishing, where she worked in marketing and editorial roles for business and lifestyle publications. Focused, organized and results oriented, Leila quickly gained the appreciation for the role media and public relations played in the development of a successful business. A creative thinker at heart, Leila parlayed her publishing experience into the wedding and special events industry where she swiftly became an asset to some of LA's most recognizable wedding planners. Over the years, she has helped produce elegant and opulent weddings, while also securing highly-coveted coverage on television wedding programs and placements in industry magazines for her clients.

Today, Leila continues to create new avenues to represent and market her wedding industry clients, whether she is helping them to grow their business from the beginning or keeping an established name at the top of the industry. By employing the power of public relations, Leila secures the credible, positive images and brand recognition in the press for clients that ignites growth and sustains momentum. Her clients have been featured on such widely watched programs as WE Network's *"Wedding Planners", "Unforgettable Wedding Venues", "Platinum Weddings" "Amazing Cakes"* and have graced the pages of highly respected wedding publications including *Martha Stewart, Modern Bride, Brides, Grace Ormonde Wedding Style, Inside Weddings, The Knot, Bride and Bloom, Destination Weddings & Honeymoons, Southern Weddings, Ceremony* and many more. Her experience and passion for the wedding industry, along with her dedication to fulfilling her clients' goals, give Leila the genuine drive and know-how to achieve marketing success.

Currently residing in Southern California's beautiful Manhattan Beach, Leila is engaged and currently planning her own wedding! An avid traveler, enthusiastic reader, food lover and wine connoisseur, she lives life to its fullest! She attests her unwavering strength and ability to inspire and motivate others to her mother, Karen Reid Khalil, who has exemplified the very essence of unconditional love and how it knows no boundaries. Leila believes that a strong foundation, infused with heart and a steadfast set of values, is the stepping stone in achieving your life goals. Her family: Charles, Karen, Jacque, Monika, Kellee, Jirard and fiancé Tony have provided her with immeasurable support and have been an integral part of her success in both her career and everyday life.

Services Offered by Leila Khalil:

"Inspire Me" Business Coaching

Looking to take your business to the next level? Not all wedding vendors need a full time publicist, but perhaps just a nudge in the right direction. If this is you, then maybe Be Inspired PR can help. We provide business coaching and advising. Our basic "Inspire Me" Business Coaching package is as follows:

- Initial assessment and research on your company's presence in the industry: *Tips on how to enhance your image*
- Logo, website, blog, and marketing material analysis: *Feedback on what you are doing right and what could use improvement*
- Review business materials: contracts, prices packages, new inquiry emails: *Edit materials and implement better systems for your business*
- Networking and marketing strategies: *Recommendations for resources to attract more business*
- Media and Press Placement: *Offering up the do's and don'ts to get the features you want*

Mary Dann-McNamee, M.A., Wedding Planner

As one of the most sought-after event coordinators in Southern California, Mary Dann-McNamee and her team of wedding and party coordinators have been responsible for detailed event planning and creative party consultation to many corporations and families throughout the country since 1991. They are known for their commitment to surpass their clients' expectations and have created intimate weddings and extravagant upscale affairs for a long list of clients, including many of Hollywood's elite. Mary's passion for the industry has led her down many paths, including becoming a contributing writer for " *Inside Weddings* magazine, *"Ceremony"* magazine and an on-air talent for many nationally syndicated television shows. These shows are Style Network's " *Whose Wedding Is It Anyway,"* and *"Married Away* WE Network's " *Platinum Wedding*" and a special segment of " *Ten Wedding Destinations. "*

As a former luxury hotel Catering Sales Manager and Corporate Group Sales Manager for The Ritz-Carlton Hotel Company, Mary became experienced in negotiations, event management and hospitality. Her hotel experience helped form relationships with industry professionals, including some of the finest designers, photographers, hotels and entertainment specialists in the country. Mary takes pride in the continuing growth of her company. What began with a few weddings and a staff of two has now become a high-profile business specializing in weddings with sometimes over 8 events per month and a dozen Event Managers.

Mary believes that it is her job to make her client's dreams come true, so more than just finding the perfect location for a wedding, she makes it a priority to get to know who she is working with so she can instantly relieve the stress and confusion of the process. Mary attributes her calming nature to her other passion -- she holds a Masters Degree in Clinical Psychology and is a licensed Marriage and Family Therapist Intern. Her work with individuals and couples strengthens her listening skills, mediation ability and creative vision planning ability.

Mary has planned weddings for designers, writers, catering managers and for corporations like O'Melveny & Myers, Sony Music, Vogue Magazine, IMG, Nautica and Cloudbreak Entertainment. In addition she has worked on nuptials for clients from Pro Athletic Teams, such as Kobe Bryant, Austin Croshere and Malcolm Johnson. It was not surprising when Mary received a call to be a featured wedding planner on the nationally syndicated "Whose Wedding Is It Anyway" on the Style Network. Each episode featuring Mary takes a behind the-scenes look at a day in the life of a wedding and the personality of a wedding planner. From flowers to dresses, Mary poignantly shows viewers how emotional, joyous, and ultimately stressful preparing for the big day can be.

Coupling her therapy degree and extensive experience in the wedding industry, Mary offers advice and guidance through career counseling and a 3-day mentorship program for aspiring wedding planners. The career counseling session is an opportunity for Mary to understand where you are at, what your experience is and how to take that experience and utilize it in this new phase of your life. Mary will direct you with practical advice and encourage you to use the tools you already have around you to accomplish your hearts desire. As for the mentorship program, it's a 3-day program where the mentoree would shadow Mary and learn first hand. For the full 3-day program you spend a day at the office, one day during a rehearsal, and the third day working an actual wedding event. In January 2008 Mary launched gifts and stationery on her website which includes The Mary Dann Collection: Gratitude Notes and her custom created "Wedding Wands". These items can be purchased on her website along with her inspirational DVD's: "The Path of the Wedding Planner" and the "The Balanced Planner". Mary will also be debuting her first book "Wedding Wisdom" in Spring 2009, filled with tips, insights, forms and photographs for planning a perfect wedding for yourself or clients.

Mary currently resides in Manhattan Beach with her husband Jimmy and two adorable baby girls Grace and Sophia.

Career Services Offered By Mary Dann McNamee, M.A., Wedding Planner

Mentorship Program

For the past four years I have been offering mentorships to novice and experienced planners across the United States. It is an opportunity for them to take a step into my world in Los Angeles and shadow me for a three-day program. The first day is usually in the office. We are here for close to five or six hours during the day and they observe me on telephone calls, inquiry calls, see my filing system and ask me questions. They get to work in the business environment of wedding planning for day one. The second day offers the opportunity to follow me to the rehearsal, watch my role at managing the event, assist me and be a part of the rehearsal. After the rehearsal, we usually have a business lunch or dinner where we can discuss more about what they have learned so far and make sure I am meeting, and hopefully exceeding their expectations. On the wedding day, day three, the mentoree follows me from the very beginning to the end, for what is normally a twelve to fifteen hour day. They get to observe me managing and handling an entire day's events from start to finish, which is a tremendous learning opportunity. I have gotten so many "thank you's" from many different people who I have worked with and benefitted from being able to see the wedding planning world through my eyes and my experience. They learn a lot and are able to take their new knowledge back to their business. Mentorees are usually either starting their own business or are in the process of deciding if they want to go into the planning field. For those with existing businesses, they are improving their career and honing their craft through their Mary Dann mentorship program.

Career Counseling

Career counseling is a great way for me to combine my wedding planning experience and my therapy background. In career counseling sessions, I treat my business client like I would a therapy client. Whatever is said in the room stays private, and it is an opportunity for clients to come to me with whatever thoughts, questions and ideas that they have about the wedding planning business. I then offer them suggestions and tools to help them follow their dreams; whether it is wedding planning, event planning, or even corporate planning. There are a lot of different aspects of planning, so I help clients arrive at their main focus of expertise by targeting what they are really good at and adding some direction. When possible, I will often go a step further and make phone calls on their behalf and help them find a job. I offer career counseling both in person, as well as over the telephone if a client is long distance. I pride myself on offering professional, beneficial, objective counseling to other planners across the country. I am passionate about helping other people because I too was mentored at different points along my journey and am pleased to now be able to give back to others.. I find great satisfaction in helping foster better professional planners in our field.

Mary Dann Wedding & Party Coordinators Mission Statement

At Mary Dann Wedding and Party Coordinators, our most valuable and important resource is our service commitment to our client. Our clients are not just the bride and groom, their family and friends, but also the bellmen, caterer, vendors and anyone else we come in contact with as we execute the wishes of our clients. By applying the principles of trust, honesty, respect and integrity, we nurture and maximize the talents of each event manager and all vendors who assist us on the event day. Mary Dann Wedding and Party Coordinators is committed to enhancing the self esteem of all they meet, supporting the light of a vision or dream, surpassing expectations and creating memories of a lifetime.

The Mary Dann experience compassionately enlivens the senses, instills confidence that all will be better than expected, and fulfills even the unexpressed wishes and needs of our clients.

Our mission is to create more love in the world, one person and event at a time!

Credits

A special thank you to all of the wonderful vendors whose contributions to this book are immensely appreciated. Their tenacity for being the best in their fields and continued success in surpassing client expectations attest to their creditability as some of the best vendors in the wedding business.

Photographers

Danny Baker - Epic Imagery
www.epicimagery.com

Elizabeth Messina - Elizabeth Messina Photography
www.elizabethmessina.com

Jasmine Star - Jasmine Star Photography
www.jasmine-star.com

Asgeir Bollason - Asgeir Fotographica
www.asgeirfotographica.com

Graphic & Design

Margaret Yasuda - Mimio Papers
www.mimiopapers.com

Video
(as seen on **www.marydann.com**)

John Goolsby - Cannon Video
www.cannonvideo.com

Special Thanks

I would like to offer my gratitude to all of the wonderful planners across the country that continue to raise the bar for our industry and exceed client expectations, especially:

Candice Benson
www.thefinishingtouchevents.com

Creative Delights Event Coordinators
www.ceativedelightsec.com

Holly Chavez
www.hmceventsolutions.com

Lacy Branch Events
www.LacyBranchEvents.com

Linda La Maina
www.LaMainaEvents.com

McEmsara Quesada
Without A Hitch LLC

Monica Balli Events
www.weddingswithaview.biz

Nahid Farhoud
www.weddingelegancesd.com

Rhonda Bassat-Rivera
www.brideideasnj.com

Sharaye Hood
www.WhatAWedding.com

Vanessa Troth
Betrothal Weddings

www.weddingvideo.com